formational
children's ministry

ēmersion

Emergent Village resources for communities of faith

An Emergent Manifesto of Hope
edited by Doug Pagitt and Tony Jones

Organic Community
Joseph R. Myers

Signs of Emergence
Kester Brewin

Justice in the Burbs
Will and Lisa Samson

Intuitive Leadership
Tim Keel

The Great Emergence
Phyllis Tickle

Make Poverty Personal
Ash Barker

Free for All
Tim Conder and Daniel Rhodes

The Justice Project
Brian McLaren, Elisa Padilla, and Ashley Bunting Seeber, eds.

Thy Kingdom Connected
Dwight Friesen

www.emersionbooks.com

formational
children's ministry

shaping children using story,
ritual, and relationship

ivy beckwith

BakerBooks
a division of Baker Publishing Group
Grand Rapids, Michigan

© 2010 by Ivy Beckwith

Published by Baker Books
a division of Baker Publishing Group
P.O. Box 6287, Grand Rapids, MI 49516–6287
www.bakerbooks.com

Printed in the United States of America

Library of Congress Cataloging-in-Publication Data
Beckwith, Ivy, 1954–
    Formational children's ministry : shaping children using story, ritual, and relationship / Ivy Beckwith.
        p.   cm. — (Emersion)
    Includes bibliographical references. (p.   ).
    ISBN 978-0-8010-7187-4 (pbk.)
    1. Church work with children. I. Title.
BV639.C4B37 2010
268′.432—dc22   2009036624

10   11   12   13   14   15   16   7   6   5   4   3   2

To the children and parents
of the Congregational
Church of New Canaan,
who lovingly offered me a
space to think and
create through their gifts
and generosity.

contents

ēmersion is a partnership between Baker Books and Emergent Village, a growing, generative friendship among missional Christians seeking to love our world in the Spirit of Jesus Christ. The ēmersion line is intended for professional and lay leaders like you who are meeting the challenges of a changing culture with vision and hope for the future. These books will encourage you and your community to live into God's kingdom here and now.

The book in your hands is a gift to the church. Ivy Beckwith writes like a friend with treasure to share. *Formational Children's Ministry* sneaks in the bad news up front: our churches' ways of interacting with children are not working and need some serious overhaul. But the good news is encouraging and comes quickly: our misunderstanding and misuse of story, ritual, worship, spiritual disciplines, family relationships, peer relationships, and community life can be redeemed, and young people can be integrated into the lives of our churches and communities in ways we've not yet imagined.

Writing from her years of experience and out of her expertise in educational theory and human development, Ivy will show you a better way and motivate you to put these ideas into practice. Her suggestions are practical, her hope is infectious, and she writes honestly, directly, personally, and warmly. We're pleased to add this book to the ēmersion line, and to welcome these very important people—children!—into a mutually beneficial engagement with church.

Emergent Village resources for communities of faith

acknowledgments

Many thanks to Sarah Hover from Trinity Church in Greenwich, Connecticut, and to Mimi Keel from Jacob's Well Church in Kansas City, Missouri, for sharing their shepherding stories with me.

introduction

shepherding children into a life with God

The first time I presented the material that eventually became *Postmodern Children's Ministry* was at a children's pastors' conference in Nashville, Tennessee. I was amazed to see the meeting room packed with people. In the interest of full disclosure, this wasn't the largest of hotel seminar rooms, but it was packed nonetheless. After the workshop I was surprised at the positive response I heard from the participants. I thought what I was presenting might be a little controversial for this audience. A little while after I gave the workshop, I was walking into the exhibit area when I was stopped by a young man. He thanked me for the workshop and told me I had described him when I described the postmodern worldview and ethos and how this might relate to how we do children's ministry. He said he finally understood why he thought differently than his other children's ministry colleagues.

Fast forward several years to New Haven, Connecticut. The setting is a seminar room at Yale Divinity School. I was facilitating a discussion on intergenerational community and spiritual formation. I'd expected about ten to twelve people for a quiet, stimulating time of sharing ideas and thoughts. This notion was quickly shattered as the room filled rapidly. Soon people were standing lining the walls, sitting on window sills, and crowding the doorway. I had to quickly readjust my plans and figure out how to have this meaningful discussion with fifty people with fifty different sets of expectations. What followed was a stimulating, free-form discussion about spiritual formation and how our churches were or weren't meeting this need with all generations. I walked away amazed at the stories I heard and the interest in the topic.

Then just a few months ago I was at a large children's ministry conference in the Midwest. Over three thousand children's pastors were in attendance. One day I stood on the balcony overlooking the large hall where lunch was being served. As I watched hundreds and hundreds of people devoted to children's ministry stream into that room, I wondered to myself, *With so many people in this country pouring their lives and hearts into the spiritual formation of children, why are we not seeing miraculous results, and why are we not capturing the imaginations of our children for the kingdom of God?* I had no good answers except to go back to something I'd said in the introduction to *Postmodern Children's Ministry*: the way we do children's ministry in many of our North American churches is broken.

A few years ago I read a book called *Soul Searching*. This book chronicled a research study done with three thousand North American teenagers about their understanding of their personal faith and the researchers' analysis of their findings. The good news was that most of the teens interviewed had faith. The bad news was that those who claimed Christian faith described a faith very different from orthodox Christian faith. The researchers call the faith of these teenagers "Moral Therapeutic Deism," and it consists of five tenets:

1. God exists, created the world, and watches over the earth.

2. God wants people to be good and nice to others.
3. The central goal of life is to be happy.
4. The only time God needs to be personally involved in one's life is when one has a problem needing to be resolved.
5. Good people go to heaven when they die.

As I read this book, I realized *this* was the outcome of all these hours these teens had spent in their church's children's ministries—in the heyday of church children's ministry. After years of hearing Bible stories, memorizing Bible verses, and singing songs about Jesus's love for them, their understanding of faith, of God, and of God's plans and purposes was simplistic, individualistic, and almost secular. Yes, children's ministry in our churches is, indeed, broken.

And I tell these three stories to illustrate how deep and widespread this dissatisfaction with current trends is. When *Postmodern Children's Ministry* was released I was overwhelmed with the positive response. I had expected criticism of my ideas, but I'd never expected to find so many people who resonated with my concern that we needed to reframe and fix the way we think about children's ministry in our churches. The seminar room at Yale included people from mainline Christianity and from the most conservative evangelical denominations—all voicing the same concerns. But as I talked with people who resonated with my ideas, and as I spoke in various venues around the country about my ideas, I discovered that while people sensed that things needed to change, they had no idea how to do it. When I spoke about developing a formational model of children's ministry over and against the schooling model now in place in most of our churches, the question was always, "What do you mean by that?" or "What does that look like?" I realized there were few models out there to study. I realized that while I had a vague concept in my head as to what this might look like in local church ministry, I really had not put any muscle and skin on these skeletal ideas.

I've spent the years since the release of *Postmodern Children's Ministry* reading, talking with people, and running my own pilot programs in a local church in order to figure out what this formational model might look like. What you will find in the following pages are the results of this work and the work of other practitioners as they explore this issue. There are churches that are seriously looking for new ways to connect their children and families to the transcendent God and to that God's kingdom. You will find some of their experiences in the following pages as well.

Oddly enough, one of the books that has influenced my thinking about the spiritual formation of children since the publication of *Postmodern Children's Ministry* has nothing at all to do with children: *Colossians Remixed* by Brian J. Walsh and Sylvia C. Keesmaat.[1] This is a commentary on the book of Colossians written within the context of a postmodern worldview. One of the points the authors make in the book is that Paul was telling the church at Colossae that they had an immense lack of imagination when it came to understanding what it meant to live as people who follow Jesus in the overpowering and ubiquitous shadow of the Roman Empire. They point out that today's North American church has the same problem while enmeshed in the popular culture of of the United States. Any time we say we can't do something that Jesus commanded and would be good for the souls of our children because . . . (cite any cultural impediment here), we are exhibiting a profound lack of imagination regarding the kingdom of God.

This use of the word *imagination* caught my interest, because most churches don't ever put imagination and spiritual development together in the same sentence. I began to think that one of the ways, if not *the* way, children develop faith and are spiritually formed is through having their imaginations captured for the kingdom of God. But the question, as always, is: How do we do that?

We live in a world, and our children live in a world, where there is much to capture their imaginations for good and ill. But it would seem that if our faith has any credence at all then the idea of living in the kingdom of God must have some compelling pull to it. After all, the New Testament is full of stories of people literally dropping everything to follow Jesus. And the history of the church is full of the same kind of stories of people being compelled to give up wealth, careers, and life in order to work in and for the kingdom of God. So what must it take to capture our children's imaginations, and then souls, through the hope and magnificent love of God's kingdom? It takes people—moms, dads, Sunday school teachers, pastors, children's directors, and youth ministers who themselves have had their imaginations captured by the kingdom of God. It takes being intentional with story, ritual, and relationships at home, in the faith community, and in worship with children. And it takes understanding the power of these elements to inspire and form children into adults who not only desire to live in the way of Jesus but who daily make choices to live that way.

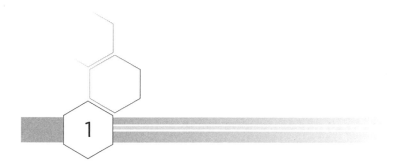

the search for a new model

Formal education, or the schooling model, is the primary setting for spiritual formation used by most churches in their children's ministry. What I mean by this is that we believe that by teaching children Bible facts with a moral application in a classroom setting, with a teacher/shepherd leading the group and directing the lesson, we will develop these children into Christians with intellectual knowledge of the Bible and theology, an emotional attachment to God and the faith community, and a desire to act and make personal choices that reflect an ethic of the values of the kingdom of God. We often use a predetermined curriculum with learning goals and objectives, and a scope and sequence that bring children through a prescribed regime of Bible learning. The hope is that this schooling will result in these children learning to be a person who loves God and lives in the way of Jesus.

Many churches don't use the *school* word anymore in describing their weekend setting for children's ministries. Their classrooms and meeting spaces look more like playrooms than the local elementary school. Churches may use methods such as "active learning," "hands-on learning," DVDs, puppets, small groups (instead of classes), and upbeat music. But what happens educationally in those settings, whether delivered by a teacher, an interactive DVD, a music group, or a wild and crazy game, is still school; it's still formal education no matter how you dress it up. Its number one purpose is still to deliver information about God and Jesus to these kids in hopes that this information will work its way into their souls and emotions and lead them to God's abundant life.

I have great respect for formal education and schooling. I love school. I have a PhD. I owe a lot to my formal education. And formal education has its place in the church's ministry to children; schooling is a helpful method for teaching kids Bible skills. To teach kids to use the Bible, certain kinds of information must be imparted to them. They need to know the names of the books, what a chapter and a verse are, and the difference between the Old and the New Testaments. It's a great model for teaching facts about church history. If we want kids to understand about the role of Martin Luther in the Reformation, we need to teach them a certain set of facts about what was going on in the church at that time. But schooling, or formal education, is not the best methodology for growing kids into faith, which is, at its heart, a relationship with God. So what I advocate is a formational model that includes schooling practices, rather than what most churches now use: a formal education model that includes some formation practices.

Educators speak of two other types of education other than formal education: *informal education* and *nonformal education*. It's these types of education that can help us understand a formational model of children's ministry. So let's talk definitions. *Informal education* is a lifelong process in which attitudes, values, skills, and knowledge are acquired from daily experience and educational resources in the child's environment. You may have heard the expression that "values are more caught than taught." This is a reference to the informal education we all experience in our families and other social networks as we absorb the behaviors and foundational attitudes inherent in them.

Or think about athletes—few people learn to be great basketball players by sitting in a classroom hearing a lecture about basketball or writing a paper on the history of basketball. Boys and girls learn to play basketball by picking up a basketball, bouncing it, tossing it, and shooting it at the basket, over and over and over again. Neither the passing on of values or learning to play basketball are primarily cognitive pursuits, so they require a less formal means of education in order to be learned.

Developing Christians—people who love God and desire to live in the way of Jesus—is not primarily a cognitive endeavor either, but for hundreds of years the church has treated it as such. The act of becoming Christian is the actual practicing of being Christian, over and over and over again. One does not become Christian by sitting in a room in a church hearing a Bible story. This is part of it, yes, but one becomes Christian by being immersed in God's story everywhere it is told, living with God's people, and repeating the symbolic acts of the church, as well as repeating acts of loving neighbor and denying oneself, over and over and over again. This form of education permeates every area of a child's life and cannot be regulated to a few hours a week spent learning inside the walls of a church.

Nonformal education is described as any organized educational activity outside the established formal system of education that is intended to serve an identifiable learning community and learning objectives. We all went on field trips in elementary school. My schoolday field trips in Connecticut were spent at Old Sturbridge Village in Massachusetts and at Mystic Seaport in Mystic, Connecticut. These were sponsored by the school but were far more open-ended and experiential than sitting in the classroom listening to the teacher talk about colonial New England or the whaling history of Connecticut.

In the church world, a mission trip or project would be an example of nonformal education. Generally they target a certain age group (teens, middle schoolers, college students) and have identifiable objectives (build a house in a poor neighborhood, learn about another culture and what missionaries do, lead vacation Bible school in an urban church setting). But like those elementary school field trips, the learning happens through direct experience rather than hearing about the experience secondhand. I've found that these kinds of experiences have great impact on the spiritual nurturing and growth of the participants. (For anyone who is interested, I wrote my doctoral dissertation on how summer mission trips affect the psychosocial development of adolescents.)

In the pages of this book, we will explore three characteristics of a spiritual formation model for the Christian nurture of children: story, ritual, and relationships. Humans live by stories—some ancient, some postmodern, some terrifying, and some comforting, but each kind helps us understand who we are and what we are for. When we chat with our friends on the phone or over dinner, we talk in stories. Movies, novels, television, video games, and other forms of entertainment in our culture are story based. And the Bible, the basis for both Jewish and Christian faiths, is a book of stories. So it should come as no surprise that stories—God's, our own, and those of others and our institutions—play an important role in forming us to be people passionate for God, living in the way of Jesus.

Humans are also ritualistic. Each culture has its own rituals, which can be a shorthand for navigating customs and traditions. As I write this book, I'm living about forty miles outside of New York City. One of the things I love about where I live is the ease with which I can take the train into Manhattan. But I've discovered that, depending on the day one travels, there are different rituals and customs one must observe on the train.

If one rides the Metro-North train on weekdays with all the commuters, one must observe the code of silence in the train cars. If one's cell phone rings, one must leave one's seat and walk to the vestibule of the car in order to conduct the conversation. If someone unwittingly has a loud conversation in person or on one's cell, the other commuters will glare and sometimes verbally point out the indiscretion. However, riding the train on the weekend or a Friday afternoon is a completely different experience. Loud conversations dominate the train cars and cell phone use is indiscriminate. To navigate the train culture successfully, one must observe these unspoken cultural rituals. Soon one becomes a member of that culture and begins to value what that culture values.

Ritual is something we do over and over again as a way to remember or reinforce the values the ritual represents. In the Christian church, we celebrate the Lord's Supper—Jesus's last meal before his crucifixion—over and over again. Some churches eat the meal every week while others do it once a month, but the ritual is celebrated regularly in most Christian churches. We do this to remember what Jesus did for us on the cross. We do this together to remember that this Christian way is a communal way and not an individual one. We do this to express gratitude to God for God's love for us. And, I believe, there is something about this recurring celebration and the familiarity of the words, actions, and elements that forms us spiritually. The act of participating in the celebration of the Lord's Supper uses all of our humanity. It uses our emotions, our minds, our senses, and our bodies (particularly if your tradition involves walking to the altar, and kneeling and standing during the ritual). These are all factors in our formation as Christians. We'll look at the different places for rituals and the different rituals that are parts of a child's life, and how participation in these can positively form a child's spiritual life.

Third, humans are relational. We live in families, and from our earliest days we've created social networks, towns, cities, and countries. We've lived in communities from the very beginning. And we are influenced for good or ill by each other. We learn our earliest values and beliefs from our families. As we grow up, the group, the community, exerts more influence on us in these important areas. So it stands to reason that if our relationships are so important in the area of social, emotional, and ethical development, relationships should play an important role in the spiritual formation of our children.

Those relationships children have within their families and within their faith communities, both peer-to-peer and with adults, have an enormous effect on their spiritual formation. But this does not just happen. These relationships need to be developed with the intention of positively forming our children.

I am certainly not suggesting that story, ritual, and relationships are missing from the educational model of spiritual formation. But I do find that they take a backseat to the eductational model's emphasis on knowledge over embedded understanding. So as you read, please keep in mind that I am seeking to offer a new paradigm, a shift in outcomes as well as methods. The educational model does a fine job of meeting its goal of passing on information. But I believe we can do so much more for children when we see their spiritual formation not as something that ends with what they learn in our classrooms, but something that is only just beginning.

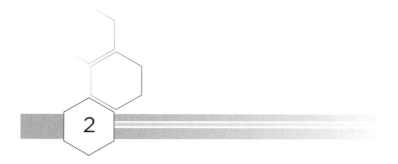

the child and god's story

A few years ago a group that sponsors conferences for children's pastors themed their yearly conference "More Than a Story." I immediately took note of this theme because I thought it showed a common misunderstanding about the Bible—that somehow if a book is a book of just stories that in some way makes it untrue. A statement like that tells me that some think the stories need to be explained in a propositional or factual way for their truth to be understood or realized. The stories themselves aren't good enough to stand on their own in terms of teaching us God's own story and leading us into a meaningful connection with God.

Have you ever wondered why God gave us the Bible as a storybook? Now, granted, the entire Bible isn't made up of just stories. Apparently the church's founding apostles were not much for storytelling, as their letters full of exhortation and theological reflection attest. But probably close to 80 percent of the Bible is stories. And the epistles arose out of stories—the stories of early churches and their struggles to figure out what it meant to be "church."

As someone who has been immersed in the Bible for most of my life, I don't think I was ever concerned with this "why" question until just a few years ago. "What's the deal with all the stories?" I asked myself. "Why isn't the entire Bible more like the epistles than like a storybook?" It could have been. Instead, God chose to give us stories—darn good, and sometimes quite baffling, stories at that.

Now obviously, I don't know for sure why God gave us all these stories, but I suspect it has something to do with the way we human beings are created. God knew there was something in the human spirit that could relate to, inhabit, and be transformed by stories, even stories conceived thousands of years before in dramatically different cultures from those of the hearers. And I think God gave us stories because God wants us to know God's essence and to fall in love with God. I don't know about you, but it is far easier for me to fall in love with a character in a story than with an exhortation or list of theological propositions about that character. I think God wanted to capture our imaginations, and the way to capture most people's imaginations is through a good story. In his excellent book *Contemplative Youth Ministry*, Mark Yacconelli states:

> The stories of Scripture are windows into the nature of God and humanity and our relationships to one another. They are stories that help us repent, heal, learn, grow, and stretch toward God's love and wholeness. . . . It [Scripture] helps us name our experience and points us to deeper ways in which we can experience God's love and compassion for humanity.[1]

Using the word *story* to describe the content of the Bible in no way implies any denial of the truth of the biblical text. Calling something a story does not mean it is untrue. Stories can and often do contain more truth about the human spirit and its relationship to the God of the universe than many factual treatises or propositional monographs. For many years the Bible was viewed as a story narrative about God.

> For most of the years the Bible has existed and been the basis of both Judaism and Christianity, it was viewed and interpreted this way. . . . Traditional, precritical Christian readings of the Bible had presupposed a unified narrative structure of the Bible. . . . Christians read the Scriptures to find themselves within its pages. The Bible presented an overarching theological narrative. The narrative framework of the biblical story itself provided the Christian pattern of meaning for all of life. An individual read the Scriptures in order to incorporate the world, oneself and, for preachers, the congregation into the biblical story.[2]

But then in the seventeenth and eighteenth centuries, with the age of the Enlightenment and the birth of modernism, things changed. "Scriptures were seen to refer to something behind the text that could be excavated from it through the application of a proper rational method.[3] The Bible became, in effect, more than a story. Theologian John Wright explains, "The Bible became a source, not a text. Theologians and preachers understood the Scriptures as a platform on which they could either access experiences of the divine or build systems of propositions to nurture the life of their congregations and call unbelievers to faith."[4]

What has happened over the years following the Enlightenment and this radical change in viewing the Scriptures—done mostly by those of us who teach and preach these stories to others—is that we've inserted into or infused these narratives with the truth we think they tell rather than letting God's truth spring forth from them for our own lives and peculiar contexts, allowing them to intersect with our own stories. We've punctured these stories and inserted our own interpretations into them as the interpretation for all, and robbed these biblical stories of their power to shape us in a variety of personal contexts. We've robbed them of the ability to be powerful vehicles of spiritual formation.

This has been especially evident in children's and youth curricula, where every Bible story ends with a "life application" or begins with "a point" for the Bible lesson. In *Postmodern Children's Ministry*, I called this the "Aesop-fableization" of the Bible. Used in this way, the Bible story is simply an interesting vehicle to get us to the real meat of the lesson—moral living. There is nothing wrong with moral living. Most of these "life applications" found in children's and youth curricula would align with the teachings of Jesus in the Gospels. But by using Bible stories in this way we tame these stories, and strip them of their power to transform us and our children's lives right where we are at that moment.

When I traveled around the country training volunteer teachers in how to use a particular Sunday school curriculum, I remember always cautioning them that a writer sitting in California or Colorado had no way of knowing what their particular students were dealing with in their lives. So I told these teachers that if it seemed like the application section of the lesson was not resonating with their class, they should go instead with whatever had captured their minds and spirits about that particular lesson. That would ultimately be more meaningful to them than something a curriculum writer had thought up.

Essentially what I was telling these teachers, although I didn't know it at the time, was that context matters. The context of the curriculum writers, the historical and cultural context of the Bible story, the context of the lives of the students, and the personal context of the teacher all impinge on how we understand the truth of a Bible story. I was telling them to pay particular attention to the personal context of their students if they expected to be at all effective in their spiritual formation. Every Bible story doesn't always mean the same thing to everyone every time they hear it. Bible stories, like all stories, speak truth to us in the particular time and moment in which we hear them, whether we are children, youth, or adults.

Off the Hook

There is no question that figuring out how to teach children the Bible in this way is much more difficult than teaching the linear way most Sunday school curriculum is created. One lesson plan rubric on which I cut my religious education teeth was "hook, book, look, took." Each lesson started with a "hook"—a contemporary story or fun activity linking the kids into, or capturing their thinking about, the particular application of this Bible story. "Book" was the telling of the Bible story, either by the teacher telling the story with pictures or the kids reading it out of the Bible. "Look" was a dissection of the Bible story. Who were the characters? What happened in the story? Did the characters obey God or not? The last part, "took," was the application piece. What can we learn from the story to apply to our own lives? What proposition about God's nature or living a Christian life can we learn from this story?

The teacher knew each week the lesson would be constructed in this way, and he had a very easy lesson plan to follow. So while it took preparation to teach a lesson that would hold the attention of the children in the class, there was a certain sameness and familiarity to each lesson. And in recent years the call from churches for lessons that are easier and easier for the teacher to prepare has made it imperative for curriculum companies not to add things to lessons that make them surprising or difficult for the typical Sunday school volunteer.

The difficulties with these types of application lesson plans—whether video-based, small group/large group, or rotation-based models—for the facilitation of the positive spiritual formation of our children is threefold. The first problem is that they are linear. The millennials and futuristic adaptives, the two generations we currently teach in our churches, are not primarily linear thinkers.[5] They do think logically and linearly, but it is not the only way they think, and it is not necessarily their preferred way of processing information. Therefore, lessons that are heavily dependent on linear thinking are not going to capture them the same way as lessons that include kinesthetic, intuitive, affective, and "loopy" ways of processing information.

Second, as I mentioned before, these types of lessons take little interest in the various contexts into which the Bible story is dropped. Of course, all good curriculum teacher guides inform teachers that knowing the kids in their classes is very important for tailoring the lesson to them, but this dictum does not jive easily with the essential need for making the lesson easy to prepare. Knowing your kids and figuring out how to help them understand a Bible story in light of their particular context of culture, personal story, and age-appropriateness is not something that can be done in twenty minutes of preparation on a Sunday morning.

Third, these types of lesson plans don't allow the Bible story to speak into the lives of the kids who are being taught. They don't allow the Bible story to be a living, breathing member of the learning environment. In these lesson plans, the Bible is used as a tool or a textbook. The predetermined, one-size-fits-all life application becomes the centerpiece of the lesson. I've had volunteer Sunday school teachers ask me if it's okay that they didn't make it to the lesson application on a particular Sunday. My answer has always been that it is probably a positive thing if they didn't make it to the end of the line, to the application, because that meant that something of the story had so captured the children's minds and spirits that they wanted to spend all their time talking about that. These linear types of lesson plans don't allow the kids to enter into and engage with the story in a way that lets God's Spirit permeate their hearts and minds with what God wants them to know about God from that story on that particular day.

According to Catherine M. Wallace in her essay "Storytelling, Doctrine, and Spiritual Formation," this type of lesson actually gets in the way of the spiritually transformative power of the Bible story. She says:

> The life of faith, the liveliness and the vitality of religion in our days, depends very centrally upon the stories we tell one another about our own immediate encounters with the incarnate God. And the work of "spiritual formation" as such, then is learning to understand and to tell the stories that will teach us how to recognize God's activity in our own ordinary week.[6]

Bible stories are all about other people recognizing God's activity in what for them might have begun as a very ordinary week. Moses is out tending his sheep, and all of a sudden God connects with him in a burning bush. David is just delivering lunch to his brothers when he finds himself exhibiting God's power against the Philistine giant. As we connect our children with these stories in all their colorful detail, as we look at the inbreaking of the work of God into the lives of these Bible characters, we invite our children to find the similar inbreaking of God into their own lives.

Nonetheless, it is far easier to teach children Bible stories in a cognitive, linear, and propositional fashion, because it's easier for the untrained volunteer to teach that kind of prepared lesson plan. And it's easier for publishing companies to write them. Engaging children in the biblical narrative in kinesthetic, intuitive, and affective ways that reflect their lives and personal contexts means that most churches will need to think more creatively about the way they present the Bible to the children in their midst. They'll need to think about creating ways for children to enter into the biblical narrative, engage with the story, and listen to the Spirit of God, allowing the meaningful parts of the story to speak to them in real and formative ways.

The Truth of the Story

So how do we do this? We need to change the way we use Bible stories. We need to really understand that Bible stories are not vehicles for getting us to propositional truth about God. Bible stories are already truth about God. Let's let the story be the story and tell its own truth to us. I think once we make this reversal in our thinking about Bible stories, some new ways to meaningfully introduce children to the biblical narrative may reveal themselves.

Weaning ourselves away from the linear lesson plan where one activity builds upon another is another one of the first steps to take. I suggest instead that we think of our formal teaching time with children more as a wheel with an axle and spokes than as a straight line. The axle is the Bible story that anchors all of our teaching/learning activities and discussion for the teaching time. Around the axle is the wheel, representing the various activities we create to engage the children in the Bible story. The spokes radiating from the axle to the wheel represent the conversations we have with children around these activities. These conversations result from carefully crafted reflection questions, which grow out of the activities and the Bible story, allowing children the opportunity to think about the narrative movement of the story, the context of the story, the role of God in the story, and the context of their own lives in relation to this story. With the wheel illustration, the children are able to reflect on how this story speaks to them about how God breaks into their ordinary, everyday lives.

In his book *Education Congregations*, Charles Foster posits a helpful rubric that can be a good reminder for educators as we seek to allow children to experience the

Bible stories through their own personal context and stories. The rubric is: "prepare, engage, reflect."[7] While the rubric itself is linear (which is why I like it—I am an "old-school" linear thinker), it doesn't necessarily play out that way in a discussion time—think about the axle, wheel, and spokes we just talked about. Here's what it might look like in a church setting.

Prepare

This is the telling of the story. It may be the telling of the children's stories, and maybe even the telling of the teacher's or volunteer's story. This is the getting ready for engagement with what has been proclaimed. This is also a time of giving permission to enter into and engage with the story in new and unexpected ways. We all get used to our routines, and any disruption of that can disrupt our comfort zones. We can find ourselves threatened by being asked to do something new and different. Children are no different. Preparing involves inviting them into a safe environment for engagement.

Engage

While I do believe telling the story is foundational, once it is told for the first time, it can be retold by the teacher or the children through the variety of activities offered during the class time. The engagement activities can happen all at once, with children choosing those activities that best help them tell and reflect upon the story they have just heard. Or they can happen one by one, with the whole group moving from activity to activity. All parts of "prepare, engage, reflect" can happen at any time during the formal teaching time. And these can be carried over from week to week too. There is no rule or commandment that says children must engage with one Bible story a week.

Reflect

This is the time for those questions and conversations we have with the children, or that the children have among themselves, about the Bible story in the context of God's actions and their own lives. This is the most difficult part of this proposed model for engaging children in the narrative arc of the Bible. We are not really a reflective people. We live in a noisy, busy world that is not conducive to reflecting on much of anything, and especially not conducive to reflection on how God is breaking into our daily lives. It is all the more difficult for us to help our children reflect on the meaning of a Bible story.

The important thing to remember is that while "prepare, engage, reflect" is a linear phrase, it does not need to be a linear process. We can prepare, engage, and reflect with kids during any part of our time with them. Teachers and volunteers need to have an ear for the reflections of children, which may happen at any time during their engagement in activities and in the Bible story, and be prepared to adapt the activities accordingly.

Here's how "prepare, engage, reflect" worked with the middle schoolers at my church. We were entering into the story of creation through the lenses of caring for our environment and seeking to gain an understanding of God's role in our own ability to create. To prepare, we looked at the Genesis passages related to creation and talked about God's creativity. Then we engaged by rummaging through several bags of trash, sorting out what could be recycled or reused. While we looked, we reflected on consumption, noting how many items in the trash were not really needed in the first place. We talked about the impact all this trash has on the earth and about God's mandate for humans to care for creation.

Then I transitioned our conversation from caring for creation to exercising our own creativity as a reflection of God's creative image in us. The kids were asked to make anything they wanted out of the garbage we'd pulled out. The teachers chatted with the kids as they worked, asking what they were making and what materials they were using. When they were finished we filed into the chapel together. Each of us then presented what we had made and its possible uses. We reflected on caring for God's creation in our particular worlds and lives, and how we might use our own creativity in other ways.

As you can see, we used a string of related activities to help the kids engage with the biblical text and its implications. We moved between activity and reflection, asking questions, listening to the kids' ideas, encouraging them to move more deeply into what God asks of them as human beings made in God's image.

This kind of reflection doesn't have to be limited to class time. And it can carry over several weeks or a whole program year. During the fall, all of the children in our church raise money to purchase food for Thanksgiving baskets. This fundraising project culminates just prior to Thanksgiving with an afternoon event at the church building. Families are invited to come and fill these baskets with the food their children's donations have purchased. All during the fall the children are prepared for this event as they are reminded of the designation of their offerings. And the literal giving of their offerings prepares them for the event too.

At the event, the children engage in handling the food their offerings bought and filling the boxes designated for needier families. Their offerings are no longer an abstract gift; they actually are involved in making these offerings into a concrete gift for others.

Prior to my coming to this church, the event had begun with a reflective activity. However, when I began to plan for this event, it seemed as if we had things backward. It seemed odd to reflect on what we were going to do before we'd done it and, practically speaking, most of the families missed the reflective part because they didn't arrive at the event on time. I decided we'd have the reflective activity at the end of the event, or at least nearer to the end, so that we captured most of the families who participated and had something concrete to reflect upon.

Once a large pile of boxes full of food had accumulated at one end of our fellowship hall, I gathered all of the participants together. We formed a large circle around the boxes and talked about why we'd filled these boxes with food, where the food had come from, and to whom the food was being given. Then we prayed for the recipients of the food baskets. This seemed to be a better way to tie this project together for the children than to simply leave after the boxes were filled. While this is not an example of teaching a Bible story, I believe it is a good example of building events, projects, and lessons around the "prepare, engage, reflect" rubric.

Beyond Application

Moving from an application-centric model of understanding the Bible to a story-centric approach involves three fundamental shifts in the way we think about children and the Bible.

We can allow the Bible story to stand by itself and trust kids to enter it in such a way that God will speak to them through it. I recently put together a short event for a few parents and their preschoolers. They were there to learn how to better tell and talk about Bible stories with their children. I just told the story, offering no personal application. I told the story of Jesus calming the storm and invited the parents and the children to help me with the story. We made the noise of the wind and used our hands and arms to create the waves. We pretended to be sleeping when the disciples found Jesus asleep during the storm.

When we finished the story, I asked them to wonder about several things, such as why Jesus was able to sleep through the storm and why the wind and the waves listened to Jesus. Then I sent the parents and the children to tables set with art supplies and asked them to work together to draw a picture of the story. The children entered into the activity quite enthusiastically, drawing their own versions of the story with help from the parents. I never told the children what the story meant. I never told them that Jesus would help them when they were scared. I left that to their own discernment of the story as they reflected on their own drawings and continued telling the story at home with their parents. But every picture was different, with each child focusing on a part of the story that was meaningful to them. In some of the pictures, Jesus was quite prominent. In others, the focus was more on the sailing and the storm. I talked with each family about what was happening in each child's picture.

We need to allow space for children to explore the story in ways that are meaningful to them. I find that children love to enter into and engage with the Bible story. If we want these stories to be meaningful, we can't assume they will mean the same thing for every child. Instead, we can provide access to activities that allow God to speak to them in ways a generic, prepackaged lesson never can. For example, I have incorporated sand tables into my first- and second- grade classrooms. Each Sunday I set up the sand table with the setting and characters of the day's Bible story. The day the class explored the story of the exodus, I set up some wooden figures from a child's Egyptian culture play set to represent Egypt. I took a piece of blue construction paper to create the Red Sea and then used other wooden figures to represent Moses and the Israelites. There was not a particular part of the hour when the kids all had to play at the sand table. Instead, after they heard the story, they were able to choose to do this independently or join in other teacher directed activities. We found that there were certain kids who just loved manipulating the figures in the sand table as a way to explore the story.

Jacob's Well, a church in Kansas City, Missouri, employs a set of core values that act as a grid through which they view all their teaching and learning activities with children. They try to answer two main questions: "Who is God in this particular story" and "Who are you?" They employ a variety of methods to help children enter the Bible story. At times they ask a volunteer to present the story from the perspective of a character in the narrative so that the kids hear the story as a "firsthand experience." Then they allow kids to engage and reflect on the story by giving them the opportunity to dress up as characters in the Bible story and reenact it.

Other times they might give the children puppets and ask them to tell the story using these characters. They have invited artists from their faith community to draw the story for the kids as it is being told. And sometimes they show the children famous artistic depictions of the particular Bible story as a way of giving them a new perspective. For nonreading young children, they've told the Bible story by employing whole body movements—children act out the waves or the wind.

The key to activities that help children enter and inhabit the Bible stories is the conversation the teacher has with the kids around the story. While the teacher does need to give directions for the game or activity, once the kids are engaged in the activity, that is the time for the teacher to begin to remind them about the parts of the Bible story the activity is exploring and to solicit conversation about them from the children.

Now, no one will ever do this perfectly. One Sunday I was in the first-grade classroom while some of the children worked on a food activity centered around the calling of Samuel by God. They were using items such as graham crackers and frosting to create Samuel sleeping in his bed (where he was when God called his name). Being first graders, they got caught up in the various items of food—what they liked to eat and what they didn't. They didn't want to use the food items they didn't like to eat even if it meant that Samuel didn't have a blanket or a bed to sleep on. The teachers might have done a better job of explaining the activity, or maybe I should have realized that first graders would be distracted by the different types of foods and chosen a different activity. In any engagement activity, be careful to keep the conversation focused on the Bible story and what the children think about it, realizing that this will never happen perfectly in any Sunday school classroom.

We need to resist the urge to lead children to a single conclusion. When you look for activities for the kids to help them enter into the Bible story, look for activities that focus on the events of the story rather than trying to pass on some moral platitude about what the story might mean. For example, the food project cited above reminded children about what happened to Samuel in the Bible story. It didn't draw conclusions, and it wasn't meant to. It was meant to give them an active way of spending time with the story, letting it sink in.

Look for activities that might help explain the cultural context of the story or a little bit of the history that surrounds the story. I worked with a group of fourth and fifth graders as we explored the story of the woman who washed Jesus's feet with costly perfume. I set up the meeting room to look like a Middle Eastern banquet that Jesus might have attended. I had pillows on the floor and laid out a banquet of olives, hummus, and pita bread so they could get the feel of what Jesus might have experienced. I anointed them all with an exotic oil similar to nard so that they would also have the olfactory experience of the story. (Of course, the boys hated that.) These kinds of activities will help to reinforce the story in creative ways, allowing the children to enter into the story from a different angle.

The Bible is full of stories about people trying to figure out who God is and what God is all about. It's a sacred text full of stories of people struggling to be in right relationship to God. It is a book bursting with divine-human encounters and stories, stories that inform *our* stories and interact with them in meaningful and transformative ways. To treat it as just another how-to book about moral living is to deny it its supernatural power and deny our children the opportunity to enter into the richness and beauty of the ancient text. It is to deny our children an opportunity to have God speak to them in personal ways through stories that have influenced and transformed humans over centuries. We need to trust our children to take from the story what they need that day from God. We need to respect their reflections and insights into the story and trust that God's Spirit will show them where God's story interacts with their own story.

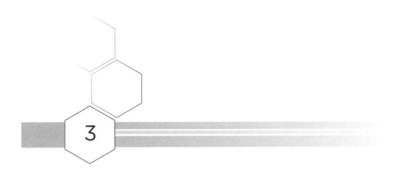

the child and the story of god's church

I grew up in a conservative, evangelical Baptist church. I went to Sunday school and, usually, two worship services each week. Somehow I grew up believing that only people who went to churches like mine could be followers of Jesus. Then I went to college.

I attended a Christian college where I had my "who's a Christian and who's not" categories shaken by meeting fellow students who came from church backgrounds different than mine, and by the school's director of spiritual life, who was an Anglican priest. And somehow, prior to attending college, I'd had the idea that once the New Testament ended there were no more Christians until the twentieth century. I was sorely lacking in any knowledge of the history of the church or the history of world religions. I was ignorant of the story of God's church over the centuries, not knowing that this history would play a role in broadening my spiritual understanding and life.

Chris Armstrong, a professor of church history, writes of a similar childhood church experience:

> Yet, through the years, though this wonderful church formed me in the joy of the Lord that was my strength, I felt like we were missing something. As a stalwart outpost of the kingdom in a threatening world, our faith seemed somehow precarious. We stood, as we faced that world, on a foundation made of the words of our favorite Bible passages—our "canon within the Canon"—and the sermons of our pastors and a roster of approved visiting evangelists. There was utterly no sense of the mystical massiveness of a church that had stood firmly for 2,000 years. No sense that our foundations actually stretched down and back through time. I didn't have a clue who John Wesley, Martin Luther, Bernard of Clairvaux, and Ignatius of Antioch were. I just knew that I felt like I was part of a church that was in some ways powerful, but in other ways shallow and insecure in a threatening world that did not share our faith.[1]

Armstrong goes on to say that this alienation from the past, seen especially in evangelical churches, has allowed the church to be "true neither to Scripture nor to our theological identity as the church."[2]

And even though my awakening to the breadth and depth of the Christian church happened over thirty years ago, I don't think children growing up in our churches today have any better knowledge of the history of the Christian church than Armstrong or I did. Some mainline curriculum publishers do attempt to put bits and pieces of their own history into their children's curriculum, but these pieces get lost in the hustle and bustle of weekly church school classes. Outside of those mainline curriculum publishers, there are few resources for any church to use to teach the story of the church to their children. The Christian History Institute (www.chitorch .org) offers some of the better resources I know of. But given that those of us who work with children in the church have so little time with them anyway, we usually want to spend that little time we have introducing them to Bible stories. The story of God's church loses out because it does not seem to be as important.

A Hole in the Story

Knowing the stories from church history is an important piece of the positive spiritual formation of our children. Helping children understand they are part of a movement that has been alive for more than two thousand years in places all around the world is an important part of their spiritual development and spiritual memory. Helping children meet and know the characters from church history who have followed Jesus in harrowing, life-threatening, and life-ending situations is a way to begin to capture their imagination for what it means to be a person who loves God and follows Jesus no matter what the cost. These brave and faithful men and women are great models for our children of what living according to kingdom values looks like.

So why is it that the kids in our churches are so impoverished when it comes to knowing about the history of the church? Why has the church had so many generations of children grow up with no ecclesiastical memory? When I use the phrase "history of the church" with children, I always explain I'm not referring to the building in which they are currently sitting, but to the people who have made up the whole church for the last two thousand years. Usually, I give this explanation to a sea of bland, uncomprehending faces. There are a few reasons for this. First is the reason I mentioned earlier. There just isn't time in most church school classes to talk about church history, even if it is included in the curriculum. And most Sunday school volunteers know little about church history, so they'd be likely to avoid that part of the lesson anyway. And in general most people seem to think of history as boring, so we see little reason why kids would find it interesting to learn about.

Beyond lack of time and a sense that the kids will find the stories of church history boring, there is another reason that our churches have not made it a priority to teach church history to our children. Much of the history of the church—about sixteen hundred or so years of it—happened prior to the Protestant Reformation. Most of church history happened when the Roman Catholic Church was *the* church, and many of the characters and stories of these generations of the church include stories of monks, nuns, priests, and popes. There may be just enough residual anti-Catholicism buried in the DNA of many of our Protestant churches to cause them to see these eras of church history as not all that important, or the characters in these stories as being mistaken in their beliefs about God. But these early characters of the church have forceful, interesting, and powerful stories to tell. Their experiences with God can greatly inspire and inform our children toward a life of faith.

Some churches may be reluctant to introduce their children to the nuances of Celtic spirituality and Christianity because of its roots in nature and cultic religions. To some this might smack of something New Age and something from which to protect our children. However, the respect for nature and creation we find in Celtic representations of Christianity can speak to children of how we still need to respect God's creation. The tenacity and courage of many of the early Celtic Christians is a model for us about following God's leading and trusting God's power. The earthy prayers of the Celts have a way of getting to the heart of the matter that rings true even today.

So, whatever the reason—lack of time, interest, knowledge, or ecclesiastical bias—our children are growing up with no knowledge of the whole scope of the church for the last two thousand years. By depriving them of these memories and stories we are doing a disservice to their spiritual formation.

A Sense of History

As those responsible for the spiritual formation of our children, either as educators or parents, we need to educate ourselves about the history of the church. Now, I'm not advocating you enroll in a church history course at the local college or seminary (although it's not a bad idea if you have the time), but you should take some time to learn something about church history. Perhaps a place to start would be with the history of your particular denomination. If you are a Protestant Christian, this will only take you back to the Reformation, but at least it is a beginning. Read up on Martin Luther or John Knox or Jonathan Edwards to understand what your denomination believes and why. Browse the history or religion section of your local bookstore or library, or search the Internet to discover this information. The website of the Christian History Institute is a great place to begin.

But don't overlook all of the church history that happened prior to the Reformation. My whole interest in postmodernism and what it means to the church was born from a speech I heard about early Celtic Christians and their views of God, the world, and evangelism. That speech led me to read *How the Irish Saved Civilization*,[3] which then led me to more and more exploration. But all that's to say that those many years of stories of the church prior to the Reformation are full of other tales of courageous people, whose stories I believe can capture the imagination of our kids. It's our job to lead them to these stories and the lives of these historic Christians. In order for us to do that, we need to allow these stories to capture our imaginations and transform us as well.

Picture books for children introducing them to the history of the church are beginning to appear. Tomie dePaola has written and illustrated some beautiful children's books about St. Benedict and other heroes of the pre-Reformation church. Roman Catholic church supply stores and websites are full of books and DVDs dealing with church history created specifically for children. The aforementioned Christian History Institute offers DVDs outlining the life stories of many post-Reformation Christian heroes. They also offer a weekly take-home for kids called *Glimpses for Kids*. Each week these colorful leaflets tell the story of a hero from the Christian church and provide the kids with activities relating to that particular story.

In the classroom there are lots of different activities you can do to enrich children's understanding of the history of the church. Let me give you a few examples. A year or so ago I used the occasion of All Saint's Day at the beginning of November to teach kids about some of the saints of the church. I created the following activity for middle school-aged children. The classes were divided into groups of two or three and given a short biography of a saint. (These are very easy to find through an Internet search.) Each group was to read the biography of the saint and then create a poster to advertise the visit of this particular saint to our town. They were given poster board and markers with which to make their advertisements. Then they gathered for our middle school worship service, and each group had a chance to teach the rest of the group about their particular saint and explain why they chose to advertise their saint in this particular way. This activity helped them to learn about the lives of each of these saints and then about what they might be like if they lived today.

One year, early in March, I took the children's worship time to introduce our children to the real story of St. Patrick. I invited a storyteller who specializes in stories of Celtic saints and Irish folktales to tell the story to the children in a creative way. I used her with both the younger elementary-age children and our middle schoolers. Our middle schoolers also watched a DVD about Aidan, a Celtic monk. We followed up that DVD with a discussion of Celtic spirituality. While it is never easy to make the connection between these early days of Christianity with what these kids experience in their everyday lives, it is still important to try. One never knows what story will capture the mind or spirit of a child or be the story he recalls some day when he finds himself in a situation needing God's help or wisdom.

At one church in which I worked, our Sunday school hour was based on a learning center model. Each week the kids participated in a variety of learning centers around a biblical theme, but I added some other learning centers periodically that didn't fit the theme in order to deal with subjects such as service to others and the history of the church. One of these learning centers was called "Our Church." One of the topics explored in "Our Church" over the course of the Sunday school year was the church in history. At those learning centers we'd read stories about men and women who followed Jesus many years ago and helped the church grow, or we'd watch DVDs about these same kinds of people.

The feast days of saints are a good time to bring church history into our teaching times with kids. This year the first Sunday in Advent fell very close to the traditional St. Nicholas Day—the feast day for the famed Bishop of Myra, who ultimately morphed into our Santa Claus. I ordered a St. Nicholas costume from an online costume supplier. I wanted our St. Nicholas to look more like a bishop than Santa Claus, but I also wanted the kids to get the connection through the visual of the costume.

One of our youth ministers donned the costume and told the kids the true story of St. Nicholas, the Bishop of Myra. Again, this story is easy to find either on the Internet or in children's books. A book I've often used is called *Santa, Are You for Real?* written by Harold Myra (no relation to the bishop, I believe!).[4] You'll also find several DVDs dealing with the story of St. Nicholas.

After the kids heard the story, they made St. Nicholas Christmas tree ornaments from pictures of ancient icons of St. Nicholas I found online and snacked on special ginger cookies traditional for the Feast of St. Nicholas. (Lots of ideas for celebrating this feast day can be found at the website of the St. Nicholas Center: www.stnicholascenter.org.)

The history of the Christian church is full of all sorts of characters and heroes who have the ability to capture the imagination of our children. Their stories of loving God and following Jesus are exciting and sometimes full of intrigue, but most of all are stories our kids need to hear to see how they are connected to that vast cloud of witnesses the author of Hebrews writes about. That connection helps kids to see they are not alone in this life or this Christian pilgrimage. Familiarity with the history of the church helps them to see that the work of God in the world did not end with the last page of the Bible. Having an understanding of the history of the church and the people who made that history helps them to see the continued work of God over the centuries and assures them that God's work will continue through them as well.

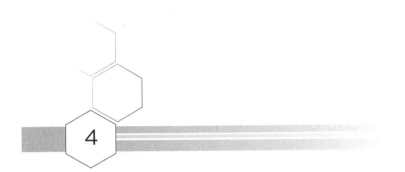

the child and the story
of the faith community

I once worked as the children's pastor in a very large church in the Midwest. This church was led by a very innovative and forward-thinking senior pastor. One of the values he'd instilled into the ethos of this church community was that the future was more important than the past when it came to church life. So at this church there were no celebrations of what had been. There were no memorial plaques, no unwanted gifts given in someone's memory, and no church anniversary celebrations. Instead, we were all about what was to come.

As I worked on that church staff this made sense to me. After all, we can't be a people who rest on our past accomplishments, always holding them up as a model of what came before. That kind of thinking stands in the way of change and innovation. We can't be an organization that changes quickly and constantly applies the wisdom of new practices if we're caught up in the past. But what that church lost by never talking about and celebrating our past—both the good and the difficult—was the memory of the story of this particular faith community. They lost the memory of God's inbreaking into the community throughout its existence.

People who joined the community never heard how the church was founded. They never knew about the former building in another suburb that housed the church in its early years. They never knew about the early tragic, unexpected loss of a pastor in an automobile accident. They knew little if anything about the senior pastor's brave and lonely leadership in his first few years of ministry at that church that laid the groundwork for the church it had become. It wasn't that we were not allowed to talk about these things. They just never came up anytime, anywhere in the public life of the church. New members to the community had no sense of the full story of the church. Members of the church could not look at each other and say, "This is our story," or truly understand how the church's identity was formed.

Needless to say, the many children who were a part of this church never knew any stories about this community. They knew nothing of what shaped it to be what it was. This community was not a community of memory. It did not pay homage to its history and traditions for the sake of dealing with contemporary life and needs. And I'm not sure any faith community can really deal with contemporary life and needs without incorporating the roots of its identity as a community into the stories of those who join them later. Honoring the past and embracing it does not necessarily mean being stuck in it.

No one can refute that our own stories, our own personal histories, and the way we tell them to others and ourselves shape who we are and how we act. Our memories provide our lives with context. Our histories help us know who we are and explain ourselves to others. Our histories give us our identities. Because I believe faith communities play a large and important role in the spiritual formation of children and that stories of all kinds have the power to transform, it stands to reason that the particular stories and histories of a child's faith communities have the power to shape children into children who love God and follow Jesus.

Telling the Community Story

So how does your church tell its story? How does your church pass on the stories that shaped its identity to the next generation? The church in which I currently serve is a 275-year-old New England Congregational church. We have lots of history and stories to share—almost too much and too many. Our history hits you in the face as soon as you set foot on our campus. Ours is a church building full of plaques and memorials. A stern portrait of one of our early ministers hangs over the fireplace in the parlor. The pulpit is made of wood taken from the second meeting house. A large bronze plaque hangs in the back of our meeting house listing every minister who has pastored the church since 1733. (No more room is left on the plaque, so I'm not quite sure what we'll do when our current minister retires.) We have two memorial gardens on the property, and the town historical society across the street houses original copies of eighteenth-century sermons and famous early twentieth-century paintings of the church's history. At every membership seminar our senior minister gives a twenty-minute history lesson, taking our prospective members from Martin Luther to the establishment of what was then Canaan Parish in 1733.

Each year on the Sunday before Thanksgiving we hold a worship service incorporating the elements of a Puritan worship service. The church staff dresses up in colonial costumes (the church was founded during the colonial period, not during the time of Plymouth and the Massachusetts Bay Colony and the Pilgrims), and we celebrate our thankfulness as a community wrapped in the story of the original founders of our church. This year as we prepare to celebrate our 275th anniversary, we're planning to expose our children to the history of the church through developing a play around the church's founding and special Thanksgiving celebrations.

Your church may not have the extensive history of mine, but it still must have stories of its founding and memories, both good and bad (my church had some scoundrels as ministers over the years), of experiences that shaped it into the community it is today. At my last church, one of the community's shaping experiences was its move from a small, landlocked church building to a much larger campus. On the day of the dedication of the land for the new building, the entire congregation walked from the old site to the new land. I thought it was significant that the children of the church know about that celebration that had happened a few decades before. So during one of those aforementioned "Our Church" segments, I invited an older woman whom many people thought of as the "church grandmother" to come and speak to the children about that day. She brought in pictures from the celebration and talked with the kids about that special day in the church's history. The children had the opportunity to ask questions and gain the understanding that their church had been around for a long time before them. I think sometimes children think the church they attend only exists from the day they first walked in the door.

So if you are going to teach children the story of their own faith community to help cement their personal and spiritual identities in that community, you need to know the story. You may find yourself swimming upstream as you try to discover it, especially if you belong to a church like the one I described at the beginning of this chapter. You may meet some resistance, because many churches don't see their own story as that important for anyone to know, or it may be difficult to find someone who knows it. You might want to start talking to church staff members with long tenures. Invite them to talk with the kids about their understanding of the church story.

Another good source is older members. They will undoubtedly have a different kind of take than the staff members. Invite these members in to talk with the kids if they have a good story to tell about the church.

Telling a New Story

Those who are part of emerging church communities might not think of themselves as having a "history"—your community might be only a few years (or months) old. But those few years provide you and your children with a history. Children in your community can see themselves as founders of your community just as the adults are. They can become excited about living the story that will be told to other children some day. Children can be told stories about why your church was started. Children can learn about the values you hope your community will espouse and why those values are important to you. Young churches have the wonderful opportunity to live their history right in front of their children.

No organization has an unblemished past. Every organization has dealt with difficult situations, even scandals. How you talk about these with children depends on the situation, but let me give you one example. Several years ago my current church dealt with an emotionally charged issue over whether to allow a cell phone tower to be made part of our steeple. The town I live in has spotty cell phone coverage, frustrating residents and visitors alike. Our church sits on one of the highest points in town (early Congregationalists always chose the highest point in town to build their churches). And the steeple is several hundred feet higher, making it an ideal place for a cell phone tower that would give the whole town better coverage. The membership of the church was split down the middle on the issue, and the argument had gotten quite emotional.

Finally, the day of the congregational meeting arrived when the membership would decide once and for all whether the church steeple would host a cell phone tower. Many people spoke for and against the proposal, and it was quite evident that if the motion passed, it would be by a slim margin, and a lot of people would go home unhappy. Right before the question was called and the vote was to be taken, the man who had first approached the church with the idea and who pushed the proposal stood up and withdrew the proposal. He said that the harmony of the church community was more important than any cell phone tower.

This is a great story of a possible community fissure that instead pulled the community together. At my church we think this is a great story to tell our kids as an example of what Christian community ought to look like. So in our confirmation program, we designed a class that simulates this congregational meeting as a way to teach the kids about Congregational polity. We have kids posit the arguments, both pro and con, that were put forth at the original meeting. Then, after the arguments have been made, we ask them to vote. Then we tell them what actually happened at the meeting. Not only does this help these kids experience Congregationalism, but it gives them an opportunity to hear a story that was really a defining moment of community life in the recent history of the church.

One question that may come up as you think about how to share your faith community's story with children is that of the difficult or unseemly parts of the story. The story I just told could have had a very different ending for the church. Would we be as excited about telling it if it had? How much of these difficult stories do we share with children, and how do we do it? While I'm never in favor of whitewashing a story for children, I think we do need to be careful when we tell a story with difficult or salacious details. But we also need to own the difficult parts of our stories that have shaped us as much as, if not more than, our victories.

If, for example, somewhere in your church's history a fight caused a church split, I think you can tell your children that your church experienced a sad time when a lot of people decided they didn't want to live in this faith community any longer. Depending on what caused the split, you can tell the children a little bit about what the fight was about. You can tell them that it makes God sad when God's people have a difficult time living together and can't seem to live with each other even though they might disagree. And you can ask them how they think the issue might have been resolved so people wouldn't want to leave and become part of another church. Don't leave these parts of the story out, but use discretion in how you tell them.

Meeting the Storytellers

Another way to introduce your children to the stories of your faith community is to introduce them to the members and their stories. When kids meet people who talk about their stories of faith, how God works in their lives, and how they live out their faith every day, they have models for their own faith development. They see people other than their immediate family who make positive choices about loving God and living in the way of Jesus.

During the "Our Church" learning center I mentioned earlier, I would invite in various members of our church community to talk with the kids about how they chose to follow Jesus. I introduced the kids to one woman whose imagination for God's kingdom had been captured by the church's mission projects. She talked about the various mission trips she'd experienced with other members of our church, the children she'd met on these trips, and how our children could help the children she'd met in these other countries.

At other times, I invited other staff members in to meet the children to talk about what they did for the church. In larger churches, kids don't often have the opportunity to meet the staff members and pastors who aren't directly responsible for their programs. I gave the children these opportunities to meet these spiritual leaders of the church. I also invited some of our teens in to meet with the children and talk about their confirmation class. I did this immediately before our ninth graders were confirmed, because our elementary-age kids always sat in on our confirmation rituals. I wanted them to meet some of the kids who were being confirmed and understand a little bit about why they chose to go through this process.

Smaller communities with little to no staff, or those that have few older people, can still invite adults from the community to talk to the children about the churches they grew up in or the reasons they have become part of your community. They don't have to give testimonies; they just need to tell a story about how they see God working in their lives or something they wish they'd known when they were the age of the children they are talking to. The idea isn't to "teach" the children; it's to help them feel connected to the lives of the people in their community.

Another great way to tell the continuing story of your faith community to your kids is through pictures. Digital photography has made taking pictures so easy and immediate that there is no excuse for not recording our histories. My church has developed an ethos of picture taking. At every event, particularly those involving children and youth, pictures are being taken. (The adult areas are catching on, and now you can see cameras appear at other kinds of events too.) Then, within days of the event, the pictures show up on one of the many bulletin boards that line the walls of our fellowship hall. The kids rush to the bulletin boards, never tiring of looking for pictures of themselves. Adults perusing the pictures get a better idea of the story of our children and youth ministries. Any stranger who took a turn around our fellowship hall looking at all the photographs would have a fairly accurate idea of what our faith community values and a strong sense of the ethos of this particular Connecticut congregation.

Last year, to celebrate the story of the past year in our children's ministries, I found pictures depicting all the different events of the past year and had them blown up to poster size. I then mounted them on foam core board and hung them from the balcony in our meeting house for a celebration Sunday. These pictures were a meaningful way to show the rest of the church the story of our children's ministry for the past year.

The collective story of our communities of faith is a reminder to us, its members, of the work of God's Spirit among us in the past and the continuing presence of God's power in the community. The stories of people helped, decisions made, conflicts navigated, victories celebrated, and of everyday life together form a collective memory and remind us of who we are as communities of God. Telling these stories to others and reflecting on them ourselves give us a continuing sense of where we have come from, who we are and, most importantly, who God is in our midst. Telling children these stories gives them a sense of belonging to the community. Celebrating these stories with them helps them to understand and embrace the identity of the community, allowing them to identify themselves with the community. Reliving these stories with children is a reminder to them of how God works in our lives and a reminder of God's forever and powerful presence in the midst of the community. Children need all of these things from the faith community for positive spiritual formation.

It's easy to forget the importance of telling the stories of our faith communities to our children. Often this is the case because we don't know the stories ourselves, and sometimes we don't understand why our church holds to a certain value or does things a certain way. We can't pass on to our children what we don't know. Perhaps this chapter has piqued your curiosity to find out more about the story of your church and to use this powerful story with your children.

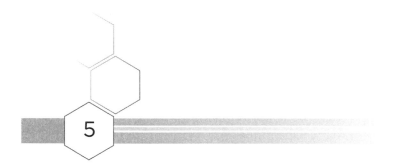

the child
and the story of faith

I was sitting in the balcony of a big, old church in downtown Minneapolis. The place was packed on this dark, cold winter evening. The event was a debate between a friend of mine and the pastor of this church about the "theology" of the emerging church movement. The situation had become almost like a sporting event, with fans cheering their preferred debater and theological viewpoint. At one point in the evening, the presenters took questions from the audience that had been written down earlier on index cards. My friend was asked something like, "Have you been washed in the blood of Jesus?" Now it's true that's not the kind of language my friend has ever used around his faith story or anyone else's, but what happened next had a lot to say about how we react to other people's stories of faith.

After the question was read, my friend leaned forward in his seat, looked out at the audience, and said something like, "Let me tell you a story." At once I could feel the large

audience collectively move closer to the stage. The crowd
became quiet as everyone waited to hear what he had to say.
He went on to tell the group his own story of faith. He told
of watching a passion play and becoming enchanted with the
figure of Jesus. He told of responding to the "altar call" at
the end of the play and of going backstage thinking he was
actually going to meet Jesus. He told of praying that night for
the first time in his life and asking God to show him God's
reality. At the end of the story, it seemed he had brought even
the staunchest skeptics of the veracity of his faith over to his
side. They may not have agreed with the way he understood
God's working in the world, but most people there walked
out having no doubt that my friend was a man who walked
in the way of Jesus.

I love to tell this story as an example of the power of our
personal stories of faith. It's easy to judge someone's ortho-
doxy on the basis of a list of propositions or axioms or rules
that one believes and follows or doesn't believe and follow.
It's easy to question the sincerity of someone's faith when
he or she doesn't seem to fit in the "Christian" box we've
created in our minds. But it's a lot harder to do those things
when we are dealing with a person's personal story of faith.
How can we question someone else's powerful experience
with God? Once we've shared our stories with each other,
we are in relationship with each other. This makes it a lot
harder to apply litmus tests of who is in and out of God's
kingdom, because we've now seen Jesus in that other person.
Our personal stories of faith have the ability to transform us
and others. We are transformed as we learn to put language
around God's presence and activity in our lives. We are transformed as that language helps us to recognize God's presence
and activity in our lives. We are transformed when we see how
our personal stories intersect with the biblical story, giving
us a powerful sense of being loved and embraced by God
as well as allowing us to see that we are part of something
bigger than ourselves. Others are transformed by our faith

stories when they see our embrace of faith in a God we may not understand, and hear of our hope in God's future of abundant life. Others are transformed by our stories when they see how our story intersects with theirs and discover a place for God in their own story.

But over the last several years, as I've worked in both conservative and mainline churches, I've discovered that most people don't know how to put words to their stories of faith. I was on the phone with a woman just a few days ago who told me as much. She said she knew she had faith, and that she spent time each week reflecting on her faith, but she knew she didn't have any language at all to describe that experience. Some people don't even know they have a story of faith because they have no language or frame of reference with which to tell it. And my sense is that if the adults have trouble articulating their stories of faith, then their kids won't know what it means to have words to frame their experience of God and Jesus, either.

Sometimes we limit our stories of faith to what some traditions call "testimonies." These are stories people tell about how they came to faith in Jesus and how their life has changed because of it. The "testimony" can be part of one's story of faith, but what I am calling for here is a much broader definition. When I speak of being able to articulate one's story, I am speaking of the ability to identify where the Spirit of God breaks into one's life on a daily basis; being able to speak to a foundational belief or understanding about how God works in the world and, more specifically, in one's own life; and being able to frame explanations of why one lives the way one does because of one's encounters with God and God's story. Often testimonies end with that decision to become a person of faith and never take the story any further into the highs, lows, and tedium of everyday life. But those are the stories we really want to hear; those are the stories that help us all pay attention to God's presence in our daily lives.

Telling Our Stories

I think the ability to articulate one's own story of faith is important, because telling our own stories is a means of establishing our own identities with God and with God's story. It's the way others get to know us as people and as people of faith. A major part of my own life story—a part of my story that always gets told to people who know me—is the story of my college and seminary years in the Boston area. For several of those years I lived in the city while I worked at Park Street Church. I was a young adult, the prime time for human identity differentiation and development, and my experiences in Boston shaped greatly who I am as a person, who I am vocationally, and who I am spiritually. When, through the years, I've felt I'm losing a grip on my own personal story, on my own identity, I travel back to Boston and stand on the corner of Park Street and Tremont Street as a way to reaquaint myself with who I am.

Most of us who have developed healthy adult identities have no trouble finding secular language to describe our own life stories, our own journeys through life. Some of us are more eloquent about it than others, and there are always cultural and ethnic nuances to our stories. But the bottom line is that we all have the ability and the language to communicate our own identities and life stories to others, and do so often.

The difficulty we have with framing our own stories of faith is that we may be uncomfortable with the language of faith or have such spotty biblical and theological knowledge that we don't think we know the right words to articulate our life experience with God.

Teaching Children to Tell Their Stories

When I talk with parents about the home being the center of spiritual formation for children, I often find them agreeing with me but still reluctant to take on that responsibility because they are afraid they don't know enough about the Bible or theology. They don't have the words to talk with their children about God and Jesus. What they don't understand is that they don't need to be Bible scholars or theologians to nurture their children in the Christian faith. In fact, it might be better that they aren't. They do need to be able to articulate their own stories of experience with God and how that they extend themselves into their family values to their children. Many parents have no idea how to do this.

I chatted on the phone last week with a mother of twin eighth graders. This is a family that values church attendance and values involving their children in a faith community. Yet, as we talked about our church's confirmation requirement of asking our eighth graders to write two statements of faith, I could tell she was having trouble helping her children, because she couldn't articulate her own story of and reflections upon faith. As she struggled to put what she thought into words, she finally said, "Well, I love listening to the sermons and I do think about them during the week." She had faith, but the words of faith, the language of faith she needed to pass her story on to her children, had somehow escaped her even after all these years of churchgoing and teaching in the church. And I don't think she is atypical of many parents in our churches of all stripes. Karen Marie Yust writes in her book *Real Kids, Real Faith* that "much of our children's development as storytellers is dependent on our own comfort level with religious conversation."[1]

A few years ago I met with a middle school pastor to talk about her church's confirmation program. As part of the confirmation experience she asked parents to write a letter to their children describing their own experience of faith. She told me that she was amazed at the number of phone calls she received from flummoxed parents telling her they didn't think they could do this. They'd never been asked to put their faith story into words before and didn't seem to have the tools to do it. And they'd never had those kinds of conversations with their children.

So first, in order to have children who are able to tell their own stories of faith and understand their own identity in God, we need parents and the other important adults who surround them to be able to articulate their own stories of faith and find their own identities as adopted children of God. This, as with everything we talk about in spiritual formation, is easier said than done.

One church I served had a segment called "Faithstory" as part of the weekend worship services. This was a five-minute monologue presented by a member of the faith community and included stories of how that person came to faith or about a major milestone in his or her own faith development. We discovered that we couldn't just ask people to stand up and talk. First, the strict five-minute boundary needed to be rigorously maintained, and we found that most people couldn't do that without their story being scripted and rehearsed. But we also found that people couldn't always easily articulate their own faith stories without help. So each person who participated in this part of the worship service had to work with one of the pastors in order to hone and frame the story. Now, I suspect this exercise was helpful to these people in putting words to something they knew they'd experienced but had never been coached in how to talk about it. And I suspect that each week as members of the congregation heard these "faithstories," this modeling began to give them language with which to describe their own experiences of faith. That's one way to begin to train a cadre of people, who are often also parents, to talk about their faith.

Another helpful practice is to put parents and kids together in an intentional situation where they have to talk about faith in God with each other. In some ways that's what the middle school pastor was attempting to do. Confirmation is all about getting recalcitrant teens to understand and articulate that understanding of faith, so it made lots of sense to bring parents, as the primary models for their kids, into the process. However, it is important for kids to start hearing stories of faith from their parents at an age earlier than fourteen. We need to be intentional about getting kids together with their parents to talk about faith from an early age. The earlier parents begin to have these kinds of conversations with their children, the easier and more natural it becomes for kids to talk about their own understanding of God and faith.

At Jacob's Well, an emerging church in Kansas City, they held a series of evening events with families where the focus was "Our Stories of Faith." At these events, parents explored together their own stories of faith and their own spiritual heritage.

The Youth and Family Institute in Minneapolis has a resource called "Faith Talk." These are several sets of cards that include age-appropriate questions to lead families into discussions about God and faith. This is a great resource to use at the dinner table or on vacations or other long automobile trips. While using these cards, kids can ask their parents things such as "What does the phrase 'In everything give thanks' mean to you?" or "How did your family prepare for Christmas?" These kinds of questions enable parents to talk about faith and faith traditions with their children in nonthreatening ways, and in ways that don't require an extensive knowledge of the Bible or theology. The required answers grow out of the parent's own experience of living a life in faith and of long-held family traditions and rituals. Then parents can turn the tables and ask the same questions of their children, helping them to experiment with talking the language of faith in a safe environment.

I've had some success with parent-child educational events where the activities force parents and children to talk about faith together. I offered an event for preschoolers and their parents around the subject of prayer. We played simple games to teach about the different aspects of prayer, and we read a story together about another child's experience of prayer.

We learned some simple prayers that could be replicated at home. Each family left with a copy of these prayers and prayer activities they could do at home. Both the parents and children enjoyed the activities, and some requested the title of the storybook I read to the group. However, my sense is that parents often hang back in these types of settings, acting as observers rather than real participants with their children. Any facilitator of these types of experiences needs to be aware of this and plan for it.

I mentioned earlier that I held a similar event for pre-schoolers and their parents about how to tell and talk about Bible stories at home. The last activity of the event called for the parents to sit with their child while he or she drew a picture of his favorite part of the Bible story. The parents were armed with questions about the Bible story to help the child draw the picture and think about the story as they drew. No one hung back during this activity—they couldn't. The preschoolers' pictures were insightful, and the parents had actually spent a few minutes talking with their children about a Bible story.

Keep parents informed in a concrete and tangible way about what the kids are learning and talking about in their classes at Sunday school. This information gives parents a starting point for talking about faith with their kids, which helps kids learn faith language and practice using it. At Jacob's Well they publish a monthly *Home Connection* parent page, which details the Bible stories for the month and the different ways the children will be experiencing and exploring the Bible story. This one-page newsletter also includes a section called "Conversations around the Table," which offers examples of questions parents could use to interact with their children around the topic or the Bible story. I write a column in my church's monthly newsletter in which I talk about ways parents can talk about faith in their home. It offers quick, simple, practical tips for parents to use with their children to talk about faith at home.

A New Kind of Sunday School Story

There are other ways to help kids tell the story of their own faith besides giving parents the language to define their own faith experience and those of their children. Those of us who are professional religious educators have a responsibility through the experiences we offer them at church programs to help children frame their stories of faith. We should always be conscious of those opportunities that present themselves in the course and context of church educational experiences to shape both children's language of faith and their ability to speak of their own response to God and attempts to live in the way of Jesus.

We need to always seek to use the correct language and to define those terms that may be unfamiliar and unusual to our children—as most religious language is. As we seek to define this language and give life to it for our children, we need to relate it to everyday life as much as possible. We always need to define and enlighten in ways that are age appropriate.

For example, years ago as I was preparing for a workshop on teaching young children to pray, I remember reading that it might not be the best idea to ask young children to name the things they are thankful for to God in prayer. This suggestion was not advocating unthankfulness in children. What the author was saying was that young children may not "get" the abstract concept of being thankful to God for all things. However, they can tell you the things that happened in a day that made them happy or the things they did that were really enjoyable. After asking them to name those things, then pray, saying thank you to God for the chocolate ice cream cone or the trip to the zoo. With young children one always needs to start with the concrete and move to the abstract. And this is especially true as we work to give children words and language to express their own faith experience.

Another great way to get kids to understand and use language to define faith or an experience of God or Jesus is to ask concrete questions around the concept, idea, or experience you want them to talk about. For example, if you want children to describe a time they felt the presence of God in their lives, you might suggest such prompts as, "Describe a place you like to go that helps you feel close to God" or "Describe a time in your life when you felt like God protected you from something." These kinds of prompts require the child to focus in on concrete experiences and relate them to God and God's presence. And they help the child to identify those places and events where God meets them. They help the child recognize God's presence in their lives. Children are better able to respond to these specific and concrete kinds of questions, which ultimately get to the heart of the abstract issue of God's continuing presence with us through the Holy Spirit, than more general, religiously worded questions.

With the Faith Talk cards mentioned earlier comes a packet called "Faith Talk for Children." The questions on these cards are all age appropriate, and it would be fun to use them in a classroom as a means of encouraging the children to ask each other the questions in order to learn to talk with each other about their faith. Questions such as, "What do you think about when you see a cross?" or "If God came to your house, how would you say 'hello'?" help children to use and think about faith language, and define and refine through language their own experience of God and Jesus.

At my church, we require our eighth-grade confirmands to write two statements of faith. The first paper is to be a reflection upon the biblical stories we've explored in the first semester of the class. We also ask them to reflect upon the Bible as the story of God. The second paper is to be a reflection upon the topics of the second half of the class, which includes the story of the church universal and the story of our church in particular. Many of these young teens struggle with this assignment. The language of faith is a foreign language to them, even for those who were reasonably active in the church as children. But as we see them progress through these reflections, we do see growth in them as they become better able to express what they think about God, Jesus, and the Bible. Asking kids to write down on paper how they understand faith and what they actually believe is a good exercise in providing them with the language to express their own experience with God. A more creative way to get to the same result would be to ask these young teens to create projects—written, musical, or in some other sort of creative medium—that express their understanding of God and God's presence in their lives.

Another church I served had a similar requirement of its confirmands but carried it one step further. During the confirmation ritual, as each teen came forth to be confirmed, a short portion of her statement of faith was read as the confirmation prayer. The teen heard her own words turned back on her, and the rest of the congregation heard a bit of her faith story—instructing them just a little bit more in the language of faith.

The middle schoolers at Jacob's Well are often allowed time to process their own stories within the context of whatever is being taught during a particular learning event. For example, recently they have been studying different types of psalms. After the group reads a psalm together, the kids participate in a time of silence during which they either write down different words or phrases from that psalm that resonated with their own story or something in the psalm they just didn't connect with. They have the opportunity to share some of these discoveries with the rest of the group.

Some communities have the children keep a journal about their learning experiences. As the children participate in a particular Bible story through a variety of activities, they are asked to write down and reflect upon what they learn. Journaling has long been understood to be a way toward personal revelation, healing, and transformation. Teaching kids this skill at an early age and centering the practice on their spiritual transformation is a wonderful path to lead them down and a great help toward teaching them to articulate their own stories of faith.

When we learn how to tell our own stories, we learn about ourselves and grow as persons as we reflect on our activities, victories, goals, and losses. We learn more about who we are, what we value, and what we believe to be truth. The same thing happens when we are able to tell and reflect on our own stories of faith. We discover what we really believe about God and Jesus. We notice the dissonance between how we sometimes live and the values of God's kingdom, causing us to grow to be more Christlike. We learn to spot the inbreaking of God's Spirit into our stories and to find God in our lives, even on their darkest days. And we are better able to tell our own faith stories to others, both to introduce them to the way of Jesus and to grow closer in community with other people of faith. When we can do these things with the stories of our life with God, we are walking down a path of positive spiritual formation.

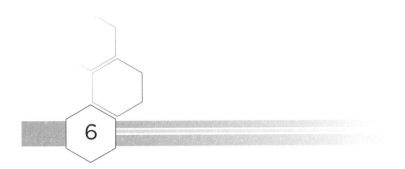

the transformative power
of ritual

A few years ago during the Christmas season I was driving home and listening to my local NPR station. The interviewer was talking to a rabbi who was explaining the story of Hanukkah and the various celebratory traditions surrounding this Jewish holiday. My mind wandered in and out of the interview until I heard the rabbi say, "There is no passing on of values without ritual." If I'd been walking rather than driving, those words would have stopped me in my tracks. I'd suspected for some time that ritual had transformative power, but I'd never heard my suspicions about ritual framed in quite the way this rabbi did. I chewed on this sentence during the rest of my drive home, and have chewed on it ever since.

As I thought more and more about ritual and the ways it transforms us as human beings, I thought about my own experience of personal transformation through ritual. After the September 11 terrorist attacks, I suffered a crisis of faith and found my faith on very shaky ground. Yet I didn't want to give up. I wanted to be a faithful person, but I knew deep inside me that faithfulness would be different than what I'd experienced before. Even though at the time I felt nothing remotely related to faith and could not pray, I determined I would participate in ritual and other types of spiritual experience every chance I had.

The church I served at the time celebrated a Wednesday evening Eucharist, which I attended every week unless I was out of town. I participated each week in the nontraditional Eucharistic celebration at Solomon's Porch, an emerging church in the Minneapolis area. And I immersed myself in other types of spiritual disciplines and rituals (walking the labyrinth, centering prayer, and *lectio divina*) as I had the opportunity. What I discovered was that these rituals and spiritual experiences anchored me in the story of God and to the remnants of my faith attached to that story of God. It was these experiences of meeting God through ritual practice that gradually brought me to the new faith in God and God's kingdom that I now experience.

The Power of Ritual

If what the rabbi said is true—if there is no passing on of values without the experience of ritual—what is it about ritual that gives it such power?

Sociologist Erving Goffman characterizes ritual as having a "key role in shaping both individual character and stratified group boundaries."[1] Ritual shapes and transforms human personality and identifies individuals with the group involved in the ritual. Ritual binds people to communities through the group experience and binds people to the values of that community. Ritual has also been defined as the "symbolic use of bodily movement and gesture in a social situation to express and articulate meaning."[2] In order for ritual to be ritual, we need to do something; we need to move and, often, do that movement over and over again. And when this action is done with others who are doing the same thing, the action finds meaning that can lead to transformation.

Let's look at the celebration of the Lord's Supper, a ritual found in most Christian churches. While the Lord's Supper is celebrated in many ways, certain elements of this ritual are the same everywhere. There is bread or some element that is breadlike and something to drink, usually from a grape. The faith community listens to or reads together some words re-creating the words Jesus spoke at the Last Supper, and we are invited to at least eat and, in most Protestant traditions, drink in remembrance of what Jesus has done for us.

Whether we call it the Eucharist or communion, faith communities do it together as a shared experience. We are active as we take the bread and put it in our mouths. We are active as we drink the wine or the grape juice. We eat a small meal together to remind us of God's spiritual feeding of us. And the elements of the ritual have symbolic meaning as well as we remember the broken and bloody body of Jesus. The ritual drives us straight to the heart of the meaning of our collective faith. It pulls the group together through the uttering of the same words and the execution of the same gestures. The shared experience, pregnant with meaning, draws the community together around the sacred. In this way, ritual experiences give rise to "group emblems, markers of group identity,"[3] or as I would call it, values or a group ethos. We are helped to understand who we are as God's people because of these rituals we do together.

Ritual both creates and focuses the group on a sacred symbol. For Christian communities that sacred symbol is God. Obviously, the faith community does not create God as the sacred symbol of the ritual. God exists outside of time and any kind of group process. However, because we as humans can never understand and completely know God, I do think this process of ritual, which creates the sacred object, does contribute to our own and our children's personal images of God. The rituals we do with God at the center shape our understanding of who God is and what God values.

For example, if a youth pastor wants the kids in her youth group to think that God is "cool," in whatever way youth culture is currently defining that word, she will create rituals to help the group view and understand God in that way. More formal religious rituals may allow the participants to understand God in a more transcendent way than those in the hypothetical youth group. This is perhaps why emerging churches have chosen to use a mixture of rituals, ancient and modern, in their worship of God—perhaps this opens up our understanding of God as the sacred object in new ways.

Another aspect of understanding this sacred symbol of ritual behavior is that it is a part of human behavior to continue to respect symbols only when they are "charged up with sentiments by participation in rituals."[4]

> Sentiments run down and fade away unless they are periodically renewed. Religion . . . is not simply a body of beliefs, but beliefs sustained by ritual practices. When the practices stop, the beliefs lose their emotional import, becoming mere memories, forms without substance, eventually dead and meaningless.[5]

Perhaps this is why when I entered my crisis of faith I intuitively knew that if I wanted to hold on to any semblance of faith, I needed to continue in faith practices.

But rituals do more than to just charge up the "sacred object." Rituals also give the ritual participants a charge, or a reservoir, of emotional energy.

> This socially derived emotional energy . . . is a feeling of confidence, courage to take action, boldness in taking initiative. It is morally suffused energy; it makes the individual feel not only good, but exalted, with the sense of doing what is most important and most valuable. . . . Whoever has experienced this kind of moment wants to repeat it.[6]

Many of us remember the "last night of camp" experiences. Often it's a bonfire where the campers relive their time at camp and talk about how they met God that week. Sometimes the campers do things like throw a twig in the fire as a symbol of a renewed commitment to faith. Everyone leaves camp the next day high on the experience and determined to make choices that reflect this new desire to follow in the way of Jesus. But gradually that "high" fades because we can't live at camp or on a retreat. But we do desire that kind of experience again, whether it is found in church participation or other kinds of ritual experience. The apostle Paul understood this when he admonished those in the early church not to forsake the gathering of themselves together.

Another interesting effect of ritual behavior that is pertinent to our discussion of the transformative power of ritual is that it can result in morality.[7] Rituals act as the source of the group's standards of morality.

> It is the heightened experience of intersubjectivity and emotional strength in group rituals that generates the conception of what is good; what is opposed to that is what is evil. Transferred to symbols and sacred objects, the concept of moral good is attached to beliefs in religious beings.[8]

The emotional and group energy around our rituals enforces what the belief system tells us about morality. Thus, ritual has the ability to transform our beliefs about right and wrong, good and evil, and put those beliefs into action.

So if all kinds of rituals have the power to transform the ritual participants, imagine how much more power Christian rituals have with the work of the Holy Spirit behind them. In his book *Christly Gestures*, Brett Webb-Mitchell says that

> Christians rituals are those practices that are dynamic, gesture-bound, participated in by a community of God's people, patterned by the narratives of our traditions and repetitive performances, and based on Scripture as it is proclaimed

and expressed in the art of symbols, signs and other human gestures that continually remind us that we are Christ's. The rituals we practice communicate God's story, which in turn determines the way we live by performing the multitude of Christian rituals. We are being absorbed into the Story that narrates all gesture bound rituals.[9]

It's almost as if the practice of Christian rituals imprints God's story upon us and helps us to understand it in a way that simply hearing it cannot do. There is something about the kinesthetic aspect of ritual that bonds us to God's story and God's way that is amazingly transformational.

Our rituals have the power to bind us together as faith communities and faithful families. Our rituals help us to understand God and ourselves. Our rituals create in us a desire to live faithfully and bind us to the power of good over evil. Rituals practiced both in faith communities and at home have the great power to spiritually form our children and ourselves.

Redeeming Ritual

A few days before last Christmas I received the following email from a denominational minister in the area:

> Dearest Colleagues: It is surprising how much Christmas is full of—well—no surprises. Though my children are just ten and twelve, they have well-formed expectations about how the holiday is to be celebrated:
>
> - A tree from Jones Farm
> - The favorite ornaments that we hang while listening to carols
> - The crèches—I have about ten, but we pick out a different four or five to lay out each year
> - Batches of cookies (we each pick one recipe)
> - A big red bow to festoon the dog (now just her second Christmas with us, but the tradition is already set)

- Worship at church and a dinner of some shrimp dish on Christmas Eve
- Stockings before breakfast in our jammies on Christmas morning, a few presents thereafter
- And a few presents every day thereafter until they are all gone, or until Epiphany . . .

Even so, what repeatedly does surprise me is: how much I love church at Christmas, how deep the joy of hot cocoa and family is, how much the tidings of great joy ring with warm, muted trumpet tones in the imagination of my heart, and how grateful I am for the people who embody the Christ indwelling.

As I read this email, my first thought was, "What wonderful family rituals and traditions." I was struck especially by the gift giving through Epiphany. I thought this was a wonderful way to teach children that the Christmas season begins with Christmas (and not Halloween, as our local mall would like us to believe), paving the way for a real celebration of Advent. And it's a great way to practically combat the excess of gifts that come at our children on Christmas morning, which effectively obliterate anything they might have learned the night before about the true meaning of Christmas. And I was reminded of the power of family rituals around family life, and sacred days to capture the imagination of children and open the door toward powerful spiritual formation possibilities.

Those of us who work with children in the church need to be concerned with family rituals. We need to help families identify their own rituals and help them understand their power to transform both parents and children. And we need to give families the tools and the resources to create their own rituals.

So, what are family rituals, and why are they so important to family life and the spiritual transformation of children and families? Family rituals are behaviors involving most family members that represent something to the family about the family's identity and values. The family becomes so attached to these rituals that they want to do them over and over again.

Researchers have identified three types of family rituals:

1. *Celebrations* (holidays or rite of passage transitions) that rise from the religious, cultural, or ethnic ethos of the family. These can be especially important for spiritual formation, because many of the holidays families celebrate connect to the biblical story or the history of the church in some way. And these can be wonderful places for the church and families to partner, because both the community and the family celebrate these holidays at the same time.

2. *Traditions*, which can connect to the actions of previous generations. These are less culture specific, because they reflect each family's identity and values. These are rituals and traditions like always having a great-grandma's sweet potatoes at Thanksgiving dinner or using a family heirloom as a christening gown. These traditions remind the family of its own story and its own personal identity. Faithful families can use these as a means of reminding their children where God intersects and breaks into their history and identities.

3. *Routines*, which are the rituals that are most frequently participated in but are the least planned, such as bed- and bathtime routines, that work to organize everyday life. Bedtimes have always been the place for parents and kids to pray together and talk a little bit about the day. Churches can help parents make the most of these times by offering resources for praying with children or having meaningful conversations with them. Traditionally, bedtime means storytime in many households. Christian children's books have come a long way in the last ten years. Churches can encourage parents to

mix some Bible story books in with the other classic children's stories.

In an article on the power of family ritual, John Friesen delineates six ways that rituals strengthen and transform the family. While Friesen is not particularly interested in spiritual formation, we'll see how this means of transformation can be extrapolated into the area of spiritual transformation too.

First, *rituals make changes and transitions manageable.* Change or transition, even positive change and transition, is a difficult time for an individual, system, or institution. The family that plans and practices ritual around these threatening transitions is on the way toward keeping the family stable in the midst of them. For example, the family who celebrates the various milestones of independence for children as they grow up is better able to cope with the changes and disruptions those steps of independence bring to the family system. Through celebratory ritual the family has acknowledged the transition, acknowledged its disruption, and acknowledged that while things may be different from now on, that is not necessarily a bad thing for the family.

The church can help families become intentional about creating these kinds of rituals by creating rites of passage for the children in their care, thus enabling families to learn how to celebrate these passages. We can ritualize the start of the school year or start of high school or even getting a driver's license, enabling parents to create ways to celebrate these passages together and helping the child to understand both the joy and the importance of the stage of life.

Second, *rituals facilitate the transmission of values and belief.* In her book *To Dance with God*, Gertrude Mueller Nelson says this about rituals: "At its core, a rite or ceremony points us, through our humanity, to the transcendent. Through rites we raise what is happening to us to a level of conscious awareness and in doing so we actually seek to be transformed."[10] The emotional energy surrounding our rites

and rituals helps to cement affectively those beliefs and stories and values we've been taught so many times cognitively.
Family rituals help children to understand and identify with
the values of the family, cementing the family's way of doing
life together in the mind and emotional life of the child.

Third, according to Friesen, *rituals contribute to building the family identity* or, as I might refer to it, the family
story. Family traditions that have been handed down through
generations, such as always using a certain ornament on the
Christmas tree at Christmastime or opening the presents on
Christmas Eve, create a family lore unique to each family.
This helps children to see their own uniqueness as well as
helping them gain an understanding of their connectedness
to past generations. New rites and rituals that families create help parents to shape a family life that best reflects the
values and ethos they want to live out as a family and teach
their children. Churches can help families develop these rites
and rituals by asking some families to tell the stories of their
personal rituals to other families. At several family Christmas
Eve services, I asked different families to share some of their
Christmas traditions with the gathered congregation. I did
this in hopes that hearing these ideas would spark the imaginations of other families with ideas for creating their own
family rituals as a way to grow their own family's identity.

Providing support and containment for strong emotions
is the fourth way rituals are able to strengthen families. One
of the reasons societies and cultures create rituals around big
life transitions such as birth, puberty, marriage, and death is
that these transitions engender in human beings a great deal
of emotion, both positive and negative. All of these transitions are in some ways bittersweet—they signal the end of
things as they were and signal a new way of being for the
people involved. Baby showers, baptisms, bar mitzvahs, wed-
dings, bachelor parties, wakes, and funerals are all rituals that
provide us with support during our transitions and give us a
safe place to express all the emotions we are dealing with. As

communities of faith partner and walk with families during these life transitions, we can help them identify those rituals that will help them cope with, grieve for, and celebrate the changes happening in their lives. Through describing these rituals, the church can help them see and understand the ways God is breaking into their life through these transitions as well.

Fifth, *family rituals "which coordinate family, church, and community values are helpful to young people in developing their sense of personal identity."*[11]

> In the Jewish tradition, the bar mitzvah is a classical example of a coordination ritual. The Jewish child in transition to adulthood takes on a different status within his family, church and community after celebrating the bar mitzvah. During the ritual he has to demonstrate competency in the sacred language, Hebrew, and lead the congregation in religious exercise for a short period. The family then bestows gifts on the young man to acknowledge his new status. The religious community is involved in the ritual. Readings are taken from the Torah and symbolic activities are undertaken which have been passed from generation to generation. Past, present, and future realities are linked by use of the bar mitzvah ritual.[12]

The Search Institute in Minneapolis has done a great deal of research on what they call "assets." These define the type of support the family, church, and community give to their children. The more of these assets, or support, a child has while growing up, the better the chance the child has at spiritual and emotional maturity. Rites and traditions that combine family ritual with community and religious ritual strengthen the child's ties to the family, community, religious community, and ultimately to the values behind the ritual. In the Christian church, rituals like baptism or infant dedication are examples of this coordination between family, church, and community. These rituals, while centered on the family, involve the faith community and can involve the larger social community as parents invite friends and neighbors to be part of the celebration. During the ritual the faith community promises to help the parents care for the child and teach the child the stories of God, thus ensuring community support for his or her growth.

The last function of family rituals is to *promote healing*.

> During the family life cycle, there are numerous important events and transitions which take place over time. Often these events are not adequately recognized. Rituals are important and useful ways of assisting individuals and families in dealing with transitions and losses, bringing about healing and transmitting values from generation to generation. The effective use of rituals is one avenue of strengthening families and creating an environment where personal well-being is enhanced.[13]

Suppose a family goes through the crisis of the death of a parent—a devastating loss for any child. In this situation it is important for the surviving parent to continue on with rituals important to the family or to the deceased parent so that the child sees that, even though his or her life has changed in many ways, the essence of some things has remained the same. Also, continuing the ritual keeps the child connected to the lost parent. As churches provide pastoral care to families in need of healing, they can remind families of the importance of continuing certain rituals and traditions despite the current difficulties. Churches can also be instrumental in helping these families think creatively about what kinds of rituals might provide them with the needed solace and healing.

Children are positively spiritually formed in the family when they understand the values underpinning the lifestyle of the family. Children understand and internalize these values as they are told the identifying story of their family over and over again. The rituals and traditions of the family are instrumental in telling that story and the story of God's role in their lives.

Creating Ritual

So how does a family go about creating rituals that will not only strengthen the family bonds and identity but will also pass on Christian values and enable the children to love God and live in the way of Jesus? Family rituals do not have to be complicated, and most likely your family already practices many of them. The key to using rituals as a means of spiritual formation is to be intentional about infusing those rituals we already do with spiritual values and soul care, and to develop new rituals that connect our children with the story of God while at home. Gertrude Mueller Nelson states that the "making of ritual is a creative act fundamental in human life."[14] In her helpful book *Family, the Forming Center*, Marjorie Thompson writes:

> A family ritual can be as simple as the ancient Jewish meal blessing in which a glass of wine (or juice) is blessed and passed from one family member to another. . . . The simple act of lighting a candle can turn prayer or scripture reading into a ritual.[15]

We can help parents think about the routines, traditions, and rituals they have incorporated into their common family life, and then creatively add to the rituals things that are specifically about God's values, forming the participants into people who live by those values.

The celebration of holidays is an easy place to start in identifying and re-creating family rituals. Many of the holidays we celebrate have some kind of spiritual foundation to them. While many of these holidays have been co-opted by marketers and consumer goods manufacturers, we do have the opportunity in our families to bring ourselves back to the original meaning of these "holy days" by creating rituals that pass on those original values behind the celebrations.

Let's start with Christmas. No matter what your local discount store may say to you, the season of Christmas does not start immediately after Halloween. If one follows the calendar of the church year, the season of Christmas does not even begin at the start of December. The season of Christmas begins on Christmas Day and continues on for twelve days until the celebration of Epiphany and its subsequent season. Some families have the tradition of trimming the tree on Christmas Eve and keeping it up through the first week in January.

The season of the church year preceding Christmas is the season of Advent. The four weeks of Advent marked by the four Sundays before Christmas Day are a time of preparation and waiting. Christians are to prepare themselves for the coming of the Christ child, the one the Old Testament prophets had promised. So before Christmas, we wait and we get ready. However, much of our contemporary North American Christmas culture does not lend itself to preparing and waiting for the coming of Jesus. It does lend itself to spending lots of money, going to lots of social events and children's programs and concerts, and experiencing heightened family stress.

One way to combat both the stress and consumerism of the holiday is to make a concerted effort as a family to celebrate Advent. There are many engaging ways to do this with children that involve some kind of counting down to Christmas Day. Lots of different Advent calendars, from the elaborate to the very simple, are available to help kids count the days until baby Jesus comes. Many Internet sites offer ideas for different kinds of Advent calendars kids can make. One year I found directions for an Advent calendar made out of Hershey's Kisses. The kids took a Kiss for each day in Advent and wrapped them up in plastic wrap so they ended up with a long snake of Kisses. Then they used ribbon to tie a bow between each Kiss. On each day in Advent they were able to cut off one Kiss and eat it. The shorter the length of plastic wrap got, the closer they were to Christmas and the coming of Jesus.

Lighting the candles on a family Advent wreath each evening is another great visual way to wait for Christmas. As the days and weeks go by and the candles burn down and become shorter and shorter, the children have a visual reminder of how close they are to the coming of Jesus. And there is something about reading a Scripture and saying a prayer together as a family as the candle is lit that is a daily reminder of the true reason for the season and the celebrations.

Last Advent season the children's director at Trinity Church in Greenwich, Connecticut, created a colorful, comprehensive guide for celebrating Advent called *Celebrating Advent: A–Z Family Guide*. The guide offers parents activities for each day of the Advent season. The nativity story and prayer frame each day, and these are accompanied by ideas for creative crafts, fun activities, storybooks, or movies that help to illustrate the theme of that day. I gave some of these to the families in my church, and they were thrilled with them. Churches can provide families with lots of different ideas and ways to celebrate the Advent season.

Last year Jacob's Well church joined the Advent Conspiracy Movement, a ministry focused on giving the money we'd normally spend on Christmas gifts to building water wells in Africa. Families participated in this together. The children wrote down their thoughts about giving up Christmas gifts so other people could have fresh water to drink. These were shared during a Sunday worship gathering. This is a meaningful and missional way to help families focus on the meaning of the seasons of Christmas and Advent.

Easter Rituals

While Easter isn't quite as commercialized as Christmas, there are still more rituals families can create around it than just the traditional Easter basket found on Easter morning. Like Christmas, Easter has a season of waiting and preparation that comes beforehand called Lent. Lent is a time for introspection, a time for clearing out our lives and restructuring our time in order to spend more time getting closer to God or helping others.

Families find it more difficult to celebrate Lent with their children because it is a time of self-denial and penitence. There are ways to help kids see that these actions are positive and transformative even though they are countercultural. Observing Lent is never going to be fun, but living in the way of Jesus isn't always fun, either.

A family might set aside a special time each day of the week for family prayer. Each day the family might pray for something different—their extended family, their neighborhood, their church, or the world. Or families might covenant together not to eat out during Lent and discuss how to use the money they save to give to a charity or nonprofit organization. Churches can provide the names and descriptions of these organizations for the families. Each decision to cook a meal and eat at home offers parents an opportunity to explain the meaning of Lent and to remind the children of the importance of giving to others, particularly during the Lenten season. The prayers around that dinner might especially emphasize God's promise to always care for the poor and Jesus's command to his followers to do the same.

Easter is the greatest feast day of the Christian church. It is the day all Christians celebrate the resurrection of Jesus. Easter is the day humanity triumphed over certain death and the power of evil was broken forever. This holy day ought to involve more family ritual than simply hunting for Easter baskets. Families can make traditions out of honoring the days of Holy Week that lead up to Easter Sunday.

Churches can offer a Maundy Thursday or Good Friday event for families, providing them with something to do at home to help with the celebration of Easter. For example, a Maundy Thursday family dinner might display the communion elements on the table as a reminder of the last meal Jesus ate with his disciples. Or families could plan a meal incorporating some of the foods from a Passover seder to help children understand the type of meal Jesus ate with his disciples that night.

Good Friday can sometimes be seen as a difficult day to celebrate with children, because we don't often celebrate and talk about death with children in our culture. But in the Christian story we can't get to the joy of Easter Sunday without the tragedy and horror of Good Friday. If your family has observed Lent by saving money to give to a particular charity, this would be a good day to deliver the money, since most schools are still closed on Good Friday. Call the charity ahead of time to make sure their offices are open. Good Friday is also a good time to do some quiet or contemplative activity with your family. For example, if you have a labyrinth—a maze-like or circular path one walks as an aid for prayer and meditation—in the area in which you live, Good Friday is a good opportunity to walk this with your children. Or you might take a walk or hike in a park or forest preserve as a way to honor God's power and creation and the renewal of life we celebrate on Easter. Think about how you could offer these ideas and resources to the families in your faith community.

The tricky part about observing Good Friday with children is to make it a sober enough experience that they understand the gravity of the day, but to make it an interesting enough experience that they will still look forward to it. I remember sitting in a children's ministry committee meeting at my church discussing ways to observe Lent and Easter. One of my committee members commented that as a child she always detested Good Friday because her mother prohibited her children from playing on that day as a way of demonstrating the seriousness of the holy day. We don't want our children growing up with a negative view and impression of Good

Friday, yet we want them to understand it as more than just a day off from school. Establishing interesting and active traditions and rituals around Holy Week events will help families to do this.

One idea for helping children understand the symbols of Easter is to create a caterpillar/butterfly tree. I invited families to create these during a Sunday morning church program and then bring them home as a way to remember some of the symbolism of Easter. Sometime before Easter, find a bare tree branch. Have your children make caterpillars out of pipe cleaners or construction paper. Hang the caterpillars on the tree branch and put them in a prominent place in your house. At the same time, or at another time prior to Easter, have your children make butterflies. (When we made these at church, we made the caterpillars and butterflies at the same time.) Lots of different ideas for making butterflies can be found in children's craft books or through a quick Internet search. Put the butterflies away until Easter morning. On Easter morning replace the caterpillars on the tree with the butterflies. Talk with your children about the resurrection and the new and abundant life Jesus brings us because of the resurrection as you talk about how the homely caterpillar turns into the beautiful butterfly. Save all the pieces and turn this into a family ritual as you bring them out each year to celebrate the feast of Easter and the resurrection of Jesus.

I recently heard the story of a family who substitutes treasure chests for the traditional Easter baskets. This family went to a craft store and bought wooden treasure chests for each child. The children were allowed to decorate them any way they liked. A few weeks before Easter, the parents look for Scripture passages that describe the ways they've seen God working in their children that year. They print out the Scripture verses and put them in the child's treasure chest. The treasure chests are hidden around the house, and on Easter morning the children search for them. As the children find them, Mom and Dad are able to talk with them and help them identify the ways God is alive in their lives.

Other Holiday Rituals

Family traditions and rituals that pass along Christian values can be created around holidays other than Christmas and Easter, since many of the other holidays we celebrate have Christian roots. Many Christian families have forsaken the celebration of Halloween. Halloween is seen as a celebration of evil, and parents feel that forbidding their children to participate in its rituals is taking a stand against and protecting their children from evil. Many churches have responded to and extended this trend by holding "Fall Festivals" as Halloween alternatives for their families.

Now I'm all for protecting our children from evil, but I think that this eschewing of Halloween is an example of misplaced concern. For hundreds of years Halloween was celebrated by Christians as All Hallows Eve. All Hallows Eve, the night before All Saint's Day, was traditionally seen as the night when death comes out to wreak havoc before the evil powers are eclipsed by the powerful force of God's saints who are honored on All Saint's Day. These two days taken together demonstrate the Christian's faith in the power of God's goodness and love to triumph over evil. The divorcing of All Hallows Eve from All Saint's Day has created the problem we now have with Halloween. If the two are taken together and celebrated together by both church and family, they have the ability to teach children a wonderful lesson about God's goodness and God's ability to overpower evil in the universe. It would be fun for families to host an All Hallows Eve party where everyone comes dressed as their favorite saint. Each person could come equipped with a short biography of the saint, giving everyone present the opportunity to learn something about the men and women who came before them in keeping God's church alive.

Family rituals don't need to be created just around holidays. They can be as simple as lighting a candle before family prayers as a reminder that God's Spirit is present. Or the celebration of a family member's personal transition can be cause for creating a ritual. The celebration of baptisms and baptismal anniversaries is a great way to remind family members that they belong to God first.

At one church I served, there was a family I held up as model for the way they created and celebrated these family rituals and transitions. This was a church that celebrated the rite of infant baptism. When their oldest son was born, they were part of a church that practiced believer's baptism. Consequently, this son had never been baptized. At the time of his baptism, he was in fifth or sixth grade. On the day of his baptism, the family planned a huge party. Family members from all over the country traveled to Minnesota to celebrate this child's baptism. I thought to myself at the time, *This is the way it should be. Baptisms and baptism anniversaries ought to be a bigger deal than birthday parties.* Children's pastors can send baptism anniversary cards to help families and children remember their baptisms.

Creating a holy family ritual can be as simple as creating some sacred space in your home. Some families create family altars where they might display religious symbols, icons, or other items collected by family members that are reminders of spiritual experiences. A simple prayer book or collection of prayers might be placed on the altar so family members can spend a few moments in prayer at the altar during the day. Creating sacred space in the home helps children to understand that God is with us everywhere and all the time. It also gives children a space in the home where they know they can go to be quiet and where no one else has permission to disturb them. This family altar can be the place where the family gathers for morning or evening prayers. Gathering at the same worship space each day helps the family to settle quickly into a meditative mood as they each turn their spirit toward God.

Those of us who work with children and families in churches need to help our families understand the importance of family rituals. We need to help families identify those rituals they already celebrate. We need to use our time with children in church programs to promote family rituals by planting the seed of these rituals in their minds through activities that don't end when the church day is over, but carry over into family life. And when our families deal with a crisis or a major transition, a great part of our pastoral care of that family may be to suggest rituals to help them deal with the difficulty.

children in the
worshiping community

This week during our Tuesday clergy lunch, our ministerial staff broached the subject of changing the way our congregation worships God together. Two days later, the subject of worship came up again at another clergy lunch gathering. I've worked in churches for a long time, and the question of what makes meaningful worship is one that never seems to be adequately resolved. In many ways that's a good thing. I don't believe that God ever decreed there is only one kind of worship. I think this continuing dialogue (as long as it remains that and doesn't turn into the proverbial "worship war") spurs lots of creative thinking about worship experiences and, lately, has created new ideas around emerging worship and alternative worship. However, on the downside, this continuing conversation also points to something amiss in our theology of worship. Perhaps those of us in the church who talk and argue about worship do not really have a clear-cut understanding of what we think worship is, which colors what we think worship should look like.

In this chapter I'd like to come at the worship question from a bit of a different perspective than that of music styles and whether a church should use a pulpit. I'd like to explore the idea of worship as an act of spiritual formation. Once we accept and understand the idea that worshiping with others of all generations is an act of spiritual formation, we have a foundation for both understanding and creating the elements of worship and a context for developing worship experiences that reflect the values of our faith communities.[1]

Inconvenience

The first characteristic of worship that makes it a vehicle for spiritual formation is that worship is often inconvenient for us. Many worship services tend to fall in the middle of the morning on Sunday, effectively cutting up the day of rest. So when we get ourselves and our family out of bed, into the car, and off to church each week, we are practicing a discipline that reflects our value of "not forsaking the gathering of ourselves together" (Heb. 10:25). When we do this we show our children we really do value worshiping God and spending time with other Christians. We show them that being a person who loves God and lives in the way of Jesus often means doing things that are inconvenient for us. When we put God's values before our own wants, we are spiritually formed.

An interesting contrast to this idea of the inconvenience of worship is the longstanding trend in our churches of trying to make worship *more* convenient for their members. I'm not advocating scheduling our worship services at really odd times to make them really inconvenient for people as a way to test their spiritual mettle. But when we attempt to make our worship services so convenient for people that they never have to face what they really value in life, we take away from them an opportunity for spiritual growth and an opportunity to live out those values in front of their children.

Identity

Second, participating in worship experiences forces us to be public about our identification with a community of faith. The church I currently serve is located in a small town (really a "bedroom community" for New York City). Our church sits just up the hill from the center of town. Consequently, we have very little parking and no hope for ever having more. Many of our families park a ways down the hill in a public parking lot and hike up the hill to reach the church building. So there is ample opportunity for our families to see people they know driving by as they either arrive at or leave church. There is no hiding the fact that they attend this particular church on Sunday mornings. (Conversely, people who attend large churches built on large campuses with long driveways and ample parking never need to face their neighbors on their way to church.) Just by walking up the hill, our members have publicly identified themselves with our community of faith. By actually walking into a building and sitting among a group of people, we cannot help but say both to ourselves and others, "Here I am. I am part of this church. I am part of this worshiping community." When families attend church and worship services together, the children have the opportunity to see their parents live out a priority of both family and faith. Children see their parents make that identification with a family of faith and, at least during childhood, will be more willing to make that identification too.

Ritual

Worship services help us become spiritually formed because they involve us in rituals. Sometimes participating in these rituals forces us to do things we might be uncomfortable with in order to bond with the rest of the community and learn the values these rituals teach. For example, let's say you are from a tradition where during the worship service all you have to do is stand up once in a while to sing a hymn. Then you find yourself attending a church that follows a more liturgical tradition for their worship experiences. At times during the service, you are asked to kneel. Then at the end of the service, at the time the Eucharist is celebrated (they even use words you're not familiar with), you are asked to come forward, and a man or woman dressed in a robe offers you a wafer and a sip of wine from a cup others have already drunk from.

Most likely, you'd feel uncomfortable in this circumstance because this worship service is very different from how you are used to worshiping. You have a choice. You can do what everyone else is doing or you can hang back and watch. If you choose to do what everyone else is doing and break out of your comfort zone, your personal preconceived notions about what your worship experience should be, you will grow as a person of faith. Any time you find yourself in a state of dissonance and take the step to burst your personal boundaries, you grow and learn.

Even the circumstances of your own church's worship services may cause you dissonance and make you feel uncomfortable at times. At my current church we only "pass the peace" to one another on communion Sundays. The reason for this is that many of our regular worshipers are uncomfortable with doing so more frequently. Even with only doing it once a month, we still find people standing stolidly in their pews, refusing to greet those others around them. Being willing to step into personally uncomfortable situations helps us to grow, and if those situations involve the worship of God, they help us to grow as followers of Jesus.

Children are willing to try new things more than adults. They are often less inhibited than adults and don't have comfort zones with such strict boundaries. And sometimes when adults watch children enter into discomfiting circumstances with enthusiasm, they are convinced to give it a try also.

A Different Pace

Worship slows us down. We live in a very fast-paced world. But when we enter the worship space at our church, all of a sudden we're not in control of our time anymore. We cannot stand up and tell the minister to stop belaboring the point and move things along. "Get to the point, will you!" We might want to shout, but are socially constrained from doing so. In worship we are forced to move at a rhythm that is not natural for us, and this rhythm forces us to slow down physically and mentally. And in this slowing down we can be spiritually formed. Spiritual formation does not happen without the opportunity for reflection. It is almost impossible to reflect in noisy environments and when we are rushing from one event to another, constantly checking the time to see how late we'll be because the person in front of us is driving too slowly.

Children need to slow down and have time for reflection too. They need role models to show them how to do this, and who give them permission to ease up on the pace of life in order to know God better. Families who make worship a priority and churches who allow children to be part of corporate worship help to provide those models.

Hospitality

Worship presents us with a great opportunity to practice hospitality. Churches are beginning to realize that hospitality is about more than just greeting people at the door as they walk into the church building. It is about how we welcome not just the visitor, but the visitor who is very different from us. It is about how we help this person belong with us. And it is about how we treat other members of the covenant faith community. Worship is the front line of community hospitality. Our worship services are the one place where most of the faith community gathers together and bumps up against each other. Worship is one of the first places other people experience the essence of the faith community.

The worship experience can be a place where we are forced to come out of ourselves and speak to those around us as we wait to exit the worship space at the end of the service, or as we great each other with the passing of the peace of Christ. If children are a part of the worship service, we are compelled to be hospitable to them, allowing for their natural restlessness and unrestrained curiosity. We are compelled to be hospitable to creatures who are very different from us in terms of attention spans and social boundaries.

When we put others before ourselves in these acts of hospitality, we are spiritually formed. The British writer Charles Williams welcomed the stoplights in London because he saw them as a great opportunity to express hospitality. When he was forced to stop at a red light to let other automobiles pass, he was demonstrating, in a small way, the concept of "my life for yours." This concept is the key to hospitality, and whenever we subsume our needs to those of another, we can be spiritually formed. Whenever we love our neighbor as ourselves, we grow in God's Spirit.

Generosity

Worship experiences can push us to practice public generosity. As the offering plate passes us, we choose, in front of everyone, to drop something in or not. In churches where passing the offering plate is part of the tradition, the discipline of giving slaps us in the face at every worship service we attend. At a class I attended taught by John Westerhoff, he decried the practice of allowing church members to have their offerings automatically taken out of their bank accounts or posted to their credit cards. He said that by offering these conveniences, these churches are robbing people of practicing a rhythm of generosity. He suggested that even if you give to the church monthly or use your credit card, you should still drop something in the offering plate each week as a way to build those "generosity muscles" and as a way to model generosity to those around you. In the same class, Dr. Westerhoff complained that in most churches, the plate never gets passed to the clergy, and if it does, the ministers rarely drop anything in the plate. He thought that clergy should be modeling generosity for the congregations by giving something each week, even if they gave their more substantial donations in some other way.

Some people are naturally generous. But I know for me, and I suspect for many others, the discipline of generosity is a difficult one to master. We only get better at it the more we practice it. And the more we practice it, the more we reap the spiritual benefits of generosity. And when we are asked to practice generosity in front of other people, as we are in a worship service, the pressure is on. But that's not a bad thing. Sometimes the only reason we do the right thing is because others are watching. But the more times we choose to do the right thing, the easier it becomes to do it the next time, even if people aren't watching. Soon it is a habit, and we are better people for it. The world is a better place for it.

When children are involved in corporate, communal worship services, they have a front-row seat for this weekly practice of generosity. Parents practicing that generosity in front of their children can have a strong effect on their children's attitudes toward generosity. I have a friend whose parents wrote their check for church every Sunday morning, and as the kids ate breakfast, they saw that check sitting on the counter. Then later they would see their dad drop that check in the offering plate. My friend comments that this made a strong impression on her and is one of the reasons she practices generosity as an adult.

Children in Worship

So if we can agree that the worship experiences of an entire faith community are an act of spiritual formation for its participants, why are we so quick to remove children from it? I know all the usual reasons and wrote extensively about this issue in *Postmodern Children's Ministry*. We remove children because they make noise. We remove them because they are restless. We remove them because we don't think they will understand what is going on. We remove them because parents don't want to be bothered with them during worship. We remove them because the other adults don't want to be bothered with them during worship. We remove them because the clergy don't want to be bothered with them. We remove them because they take up valuable seats in our worship space. But by prohibiting children from the worship of their faith community we are, in effect, prohibiting them from an important piece of their spiritual development and denying them the opportunity to learn how to worship God in the tradition of their community.

Like adults, children are spiritually formed when they learn that following Jesus is not always convenient. Children are spiritually formed when they practice rituals and rites that both pass on the values of Jesus and push them out of their comfort zones. Children are spiritually formed when they observe their parents and the other adults of the faith community practicing the worship of God. And children teach us about worship and help us to reframe our understanding of what is happening in our worship services.

The senior minister at my church complained to me after last year's family Christmas Eve service that I should not have had our children's music director stand so far under the balcony during her solo. Later I heard from a dad who was at the service with his family that his second-grade daughter had leaned over to him during this solo and said, "Dad, she's not very good." This puzzled the dad, because he thought she had a beautiful voice. But his daughter quickly added, "She's awesome." It didn't matter to this little girl that the soloist was not standing in exactly the right place. Children have an exceptional talent for helping us to understand what is really important in worship and in life.

A few years ago the movie *Finding Neverland* was released around Christmastime. It is the story of J. M. Barrie, the author of *Peter Pan*, and includes the story of the staging of the play for the first time. Barrie had held back twenty-five tickets from opening night and was berated by his producer for doing that. The producer demanded to know who those tickets were for, since they were not going to paying customers. The scene switches to a group of orphans walking down the street toward the theater. The camera follows these children as they walk into the theater and take their seats with the well-dressed adults.

As the children take their seats, the adults look askance at them, possibly worried about spending their evening at the theater with a group of urchins. The curtain rises and the play begins. The children are immediately captured by the fantasy, laughing heartily at what is happening on the stage. The adults seem a little confused and put off at first. Then the camera shows the adults watching the children enjoying the performance, which causes them to lighten up and begin to laugh at what is happening on stage as well. As I sat in the darkened theater watching the film, I thought about how that is so like what happens when we invite children into our worship services. At first adults are put off and afraid of how the children will act, but soon the children have shown the adults deeper ways to worship God.

Involving children in the worshiping life of the community does not mean we need to dumb down our worship or change the flow of the service. Children understand far more than we know, and the simple presence of children in worship is far more important than whether they understand everything that is said or done.

Making Children's Worship Work

I am also a believer in age-appropriate worship for children. I think this is the place where one can experiment with lots of ideas in creating worship experiences. This is the place where we can expand our definitions of the mores and practices of worship. This might be the place where the phrase "a little child shall lead them" might really ring true in the church world.

Over the last couple of years, I've had the opportunity to experiment monthly with age-appropriate worship for elementary and middle school–age children. Following are a few suggestions based on my experiences.

First, make the worship experience as visual as possible. A few years ago I was coteaching a confirmation class at my church. We were discussing God's creative act of bringing our world into being. The kids in the class were somewhat engaged in this discussion, but mostly they were slumped down in their chairs and restless. Then my coteacher flashed some artistic representations of creation on a screen. They immediately sat up in their chairs and focused on the pictures in front of them. I remarked to another adult in the class, "They really are postliterate." I didn't mean they weren't literate; these kids could all read and write well. What I meant was that they preferred to take in information visually. Over and over again as I've used visuals in age-appropriate worship, I've seen the kids more and more engaged.

Second, find places to use spiritual practices in your children's worship. At my church, we've prayed and meditated. We've practiced lectio divina. I've used drama and storytelling. Our children have recited litanies and participated in ancient liturgy. Our chapel has been decorated with palm trees for Palm Sunday and illuminated with the light of countless candles. We've sung hymns and praise choruses, and this year we're going to try dancing.

Third, provide worship experiences for children that help them enter into the Bible story, or biblical concept around which the worship service is built, in a concrete way. For example, this past February for Candlemas (the celebration of when Jesus was presented in the temple to Simeon and Anna) I set up luminaries along the hallway the children passed through on their way to the chapel. In the front of the chapel, I set up lots of white candles of different sizes and lit them all. I told the kids the story of Anna and Simeon. Each of the children got a noisemaker like one would use at a birthday party or on New Year's Eve. Because the presentation of Jesus to Anna and Simeon was the experience of a lifetime for these elder Jews, we blew the noisemakers several times as a way to celebrate the coming of the Messiah.

A few weeks ago we celebrated the Pentecost story in worship with our middle schoolers. We set up the chapel with two fans up front and hung red streamers from the fans so they would blow out when the fans were turned on. We talked with the kids about the story of Pentecost and discussed how the Holy Spirit can be compared to the wind. I led them through a short lectio divina, asking them to center in on a dream they had for themselves or for the world. I invited them to come up to the front, where I drew crosses on their wrists with oil and asked God's Spirit to grant them their dreams. Then they were to go to the fans to dry the oil as another means of injecting the Holy Spirit into the experience. Both of these examples engaged most of the senses and provided visual, tactile, and kinesthetic ways for the children to engage with God's story and to experience the worship of God.

In our churches, we need to expand our view of worship for both children and adults in order to create experiences that are meaningful and worshipful for this generation and the ones that follow. The experience of worship can be a powerful vehicle for spiritual formation as we come to experience God and each other in new and profound ways.

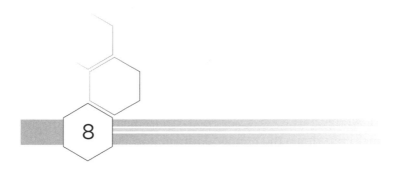

facilitating spiritual formation through spiritual disciplines

"I can't believe they were actually quiet through that activity." These were the words of a Sunday school teacher of fifth grade boys after I'd led them through a guided meditation as a part of a children's worship service. If I'd been entirely candid with him, I would have said, "I can't believe they were quiet through the activity, either." But the truth was they were not only quiet—they were engaged in it, as their reflections on the activity proved.

Taking my fifth and sixth graders through this meditation was, indeed, an experiment on my part. I was fairly sure the girls would respond well and become engaged in the meditation, but I was not at all sure how the boys would respond. As they reflected on the ways they'd met God during this meditation, their responses exceeded my expectations. I was more than pleased, and thought this experience bolstered my theories that these kids craved quiet and reflection, and that they were capable of participating meaningfully in spiritual disciplines.

I try to get to the gym three or four times a week. ("Try" is the operative word in that sentence.) But what I find is that the more I force myself to go, the easier it becomes, and I begin to see the benefits of the exercise in my body and affect. Just as we need to exercise our minds and bodies to keep them strong and healthy, we need to exercise our souls too. And just as it takes personal discipline to get up off the couch, put down the remote control, and go out for a walk or get on the elliptical trainer, it takes personal discipline to set aside time to meditate on Scripture, pray, fast, or rest in God. These are the ways we exercise our soul muscles and make them stronger. These are the ways we draw closer to God and find our lives conforming more to the way of Jesus. And just as we try to form in our children habits of reading, exercise, or healthy eating when they are young, we should be forging spiritual habits and disciplines in them as well.

Mindful Meditation

Many of the traditional spiritual disciplines can be practiced meaningfully by children. Let's talk first about meditation. When I was younger, meditation had a bad reputation in church circles. It had come to the forefront of culture through a burgeoning interest in Eastern religions. Many Christians believed it was wrong because of that association and because they thought it involved emptying one's mind, allowing "evil" to come in and take over. What got lost in all that concern was the fact that lovers of God and followers of Jesus had been meditating for thousands of years.

Scripture talks about meditating on God's Word. Recently, as the traditional spiritual disciplines have gained more favor in the Christian church, a different understanding of meditation has begun to take hold. In his classic book *Celebration of Discipline*, author Richard Foster describes meditation as entering into a friendship with Jesus and God. When we meditate, we assent that God is continually speaking to us as we seek to listen to God. In meditation we enter into God's presence and allow our imaginations to be sanctified.

There are several traditional ways of entering into meditation, into the presence of God, and allowing God's voice to speak to us. First, we can meditate on Scripture. This is different from Bible study in that it is, according to Foster, "internalizing and personalizing the passage."[1] When we meditate on Scripture, we enter into the passage as active participants, not outside observers trying to ascertain a universal meaning for the passage.

One of the oldest, better-known, and currently most popular methods of meditating on Scripture is called *lectio divina*. Lectio divina is an ancient practice of praying the Scripture by focusing on specific words or phrases in a passage. As one centers in on these words and phrases, one opens oneself to hearing God.

A second form of meditation is called "centering down."[2] This a time when we allow ourselves to be in quiet, become quiet, and allow the mind to become centered on God. Often this state can be achieved by saying a meditative prayer over and over again. For example, one might use the Jesus Prayer: "Jesus Christ, Son of God, have mercy on me a sinner." This could be accompanied by intentional breathing, allowing the prayer to enter into a sense of calm, and allowing the person to enter the presence of God. Another appropriate prayer for "centering down" is "Abba, I belong to you." Inhale on "Abba" and exhale on "I belong to you." Last summer I taught a group of children how to do centering prayer. They loved it. They talked about how the activity helped them feel relaxed and made them feel closer to God.

Sometimes adding a physical activity to the breathing and praying can help the person praying enter into a meditative state. For example, I sometimes use a prayer rope. As one fingers each knot in the rope, one prays the Jesus prayer. When one gets to the cross at the end, one says the Lord's Prayer and then moves back to the Jesus prayer. Praying with Rosary beads can have the same effect. Using these with children gives them the opportunity for some movement while practicing prayer.

A third type of meditation is to meditate upon creation. I find it is easy to ignore the beauty of God's world that continually surrounds me. As I write this, it is spring in the Northeast. The daffodils and tulips are blooming, and all the flowering trees are in full bloom. It's so easy to take this beauty for granted. Yesterday I was driving with a friend through some back roads surrounded by flowers and trees, and I had to intentionally remind myself to look at them. Soon those flowers will fade from the trees and I'll have to wait until next spring to see them again.

When I lived in Colorado, my route to work each morning took me toward the front range of the Rocky Mountains. But after a while, I ceased to see it. I needed to remind myself to look at the beauty of those mountains each morning. Yet it's through nature that we see the creativity, imagination, and love of God for this world right in front of us. What better way is there, really, to enter into the presence of God than out in the world God created? But just as we need to remind ourselves sometimes of God's beauty that surrounds us, we need to remind our children to do this too. And we need to talk with them about the God who created it. We can do this through involving kids in formation activities that take place outside. For example, we have a children's prayer garden on our church campus. Sometimes teachers will take their kids out to the garden for their prayer time. This provides them with a quiet, beautiful place to pray. The kids are surrounded by God's creation in the garden. But you don't have to have a prayer garden to do this. Taking the kids outside the building or to a nearby park could provide the same type of environment.

And we can enter God's presence through guided meditation. Guided meditation is an activity in which a leader guides a group through a verbal picture of meeting with God and Jesus. As the leader speaks, the individuals in the group imagine in their minds the scene the leader is describing. The meditation I wrote about at the beginning of this chapter had the participants meeting with Jesus on the beach and had them imagine what Jesus would say if he spoke to them. I asked the kids to get into a comfortable position and to close their eyes. I asked them to imagine themselves walking along a beach and to imagine Jesus meeting them. I asked them to think about what Jesus might say to them and what they would want to say to Jesus. After the meditation was finished, we talked about what they had seen during the meditation and reflected upon what Jesus said to each of them.

I think one of the important things about practicing meditation, and teaching our kids to practice meditation, is that it has to be done in quiet. We live in a very noisy world, and our kids are rarely quiet or in quiet. It's impossible to hear God's voice and reflect on it in noisy environments. I think there are some adults out there who don't think kids can or want to "do" silence. Well, they can do silence, and enjoy it when it is offered to them. When I led that meditation recounted at the beginning of this chapter, every child participated. That's what so amazed this teacher.

Practicing Prayer

Closely related to the discipline of meditation is the discipline of prayer. I think we do a pretty good job of talking with kids in the church about prayer, but I'm not sure we do as well in offering them the experience of prayer or in teaching them all aspects of it. Sometimes prayer gets the short end of the stick in the church classroom. This happens either because the teacher or volunteer is uncomfortable praying with the children, or because we simply run out of time and prayer isn't always on the top of the priority list of how we use that forty-five to ninety minutes each week. Sometimes we give kids the idea that prayer is only about asking God for things, which casts God in the role of the fairy godmother or the magic genie in the bottle. We don't always give kids the language for prayer.

For example, we may ask a young child to pray a prayer of thankfulness. But thankfulness is an abstract concept that a young child may not yet fully understand. How much better it would be to ask the child what she did this week that she really enjoyed. When the child names these experiences, remind the child that God is happy when the child does things she enjoys. Then suggest that she pray and tell God about these wonderful experiences. Slowly the child will begin to understand the abstract concept of praying with gratitude.

The best way to teach kids about prayer is to allow them to experience it. After all, like most of the spiritual disciplines, prayer is something one does rather than learns about intellectually. This means that prayer needs to be sprinkled throughout the child's experience each time the child is at church, rather than just relegated to a particular time during the class. As children are involved in activities and talking together, teachers can suggest they bring God into their conversations through thankfulness, praise, or petition. This teaches kids that God is with them in all parts of their lives all the time.

At Jacob's Well, prayer time is an intentional part of each session with children. Each week they vary the way they invite children to enter into prayer. Sometimes they focus on physical prayer positions. (A good book to help you lead children through a variety of prayer postures is *Body Prayer* by Doug Pagitt and Kathryn Prill.) Other weeks the children work on their prayer journals and write notes to God. And at other times they practice listening prayer and the examen. (The examen is a spiritual exercise in which we express to each other what has been good or difficult about our life experiences over a given time, and then take time to invite God into both the good and the difficult.)

Focused Fasting

A third spiritual discipline we can teach and practice with children is the discipline of fasting. You may be saying, "Wait a minute—we don't want to teach children to go without food. What about the problem of eating disorders?" I would agree with you, but we need to broaden our definition of fasting beyond the idea of going without food for spiritual formation purposes.

When I teach about Lent with children, we always talk about the idea of giving something up. I explain to the children that this is a type of fast. This fast allows them to re-prioritize their time for six weeks or save up more money to give to others. Many of the children we work with in our churches hardly ever have to go without anything. So the idea of intentionally giving something up for a period of time, such as eating potato chips or watching a favorite television program, is a new concept for them. Not only do we need to talk with them about what they are giving up, but we need to talk with them about what will replace that activity.

Both the act of giving up and the acts that replace the foresworn activity are means of spiritual growth and formation. This helps kids understand how giving up something is helpful to them—otherwise it can just seem like meaningless deprivation to them. So if a child decides to give up watching a favorite television program for a couple of weeks to strengthen those spiritual sacrifice muscles, we need to help them find something spiritually forming with which to replace it. For example, we could suggest books that teach about faith principles or tell the stories of other people of faith. Or we could provide a service project for the child to do during that time when she would ordinarily be watching that television program. Or the child could use that money he usually spends on snacks and plan to give it to a church project or another charity.

If we are serious about teaching children about the spiritual discipline of fasting, it is important to have parents on board with this. Generally, most types of things kids choose to fast from will have some sort of effect on the rest of the family. Parents, and perhaps the other children in the family, need to be ready to live with and support the child through some of these sacrifices. Without parental support, the child will find it difficult to keep up the fast for even a short period of time.

As kids get older, we can begin to teach them about the traditional Christian fast from food that we usually think of when we think of fasting. For older children, missing a meal will not be harmful nutritionally, and middle schoolers can fast longer than that. World Vision's 30 Hour Famine is a great way to introduce older children to the idea of fasting while filling that time with prayer, worship, service, and gifts to the poorer regions of our world. And they experience the fast with their peers, so they feel that support from each other as they go without eating for the thirty hours.

Starting Simplicity

A spiritual discipline closely related to the discipline of fasting is the spiritual discipline of simplicity. We don't live in a simple world and neither do our kids, so teaching them about the spiritual value of simplicity can be a difficult task. We can truly practice the outward spiritual discipline of simplicity when we realize that our hope for the abundant life Jesus promised is not found in things or status or designer labels, but in centering our lives on God and working with God to bring about God's kingdom. Unfortunately, our kids and our families don't live in a world or culture that believes this.

We live in a world where possessions, jobs, body shape, status, and house size have become our gods and the kingdoms we serve. I recently hosted a book group for parents in my church on teaching our kids about money, materialism, and gratitude. The stories these moms told me were eye-opening. A couple of moms sent their daughters to private school where uniforms were required. However, these girls still found ways to broadcast status through their clothes. Despite the uniforms, they were able to exhibit personal style through the shoes they wore. The "have-to-have shoes" for girls at both of these private schools were designer flats with a price tag that started at $200 to $250.

A couple of other moms spoke to the continuing "Ugg" phenomenon. For those of you who don't know, Uggs are sheepskin shearling boots and shoes (in many styles, sizes, and colors) imported from Australia. The cost of these boots starts at about $200. In my town, they are the required winter footwear for young girls. One mom tried to hold the line and bought her daughter less expensive boots. The first day she wore them to school, she was immediately told that they weren't Uggs, so she never wanted to wear them again. Another mom in the group had tried to at least stem the Ugg problem by telling her third-grade daughter that she couldn't have them until her feet stopped growing. I live in a very affluent part of the country, but I'm sure that in other parts of the country if it's not Uggs and designer ballet flats, it's something else kids absolutely have to have or their lives will be a complete waste. It's difficult as parents and spiritual caretakers to stem this compulsion to material excess and point out that stuff is just stuff, not the essence of life.

Part of the problem of the overcomplicated lives of our kids is the parents. We live in an economy fueled by consumerism, and it's very hard for any family to swim against this prevailing culture. It's difficult socially to drive an older or cheaper car when it seems everyone else has a newer, sleeker luxury model. It's difficult to buy your kids clothes at yard sales and resale shops when all their friends have the newest styles from the mall. And it's difficult to explain to your kids why this life of simplicity is a value for you, especially when you might have an income that would allow a newer car or an outfit from the mall.

Our churches and our children's ministries are part of the problem as well. Most churches and children's ministries I've observed don't live by the discipline and practice of simplicity. As more and more churches are compelled to be attractional rather than missional, buildings become more and more expansive and expensive to keep up. We develop more and more programs to keep more and more people busy, which costs the church more money, which means we need to entice more people to give more money. We turn our ministers into program directors. We turn our children's ministry areas into amusement parks that cost millions of dollars. What kind of message about service to God and kingdom do we send to our kids when our churches have become the places of excess many of them are?

I'm not suggesting that churches should meet in tents or that we should not be concerned about having a welcoming, child-friendly environment for our children. What I am suggesting is that we look at much of what we do through the grid of simplicity—that we ask ourselves why we are starting a particular program or buying this piece of equipment. Will this truly contribute to the spiritual formation of children, or are we doing this simply to be like the larger church down the road? Will this plan help to capture our kid's imaginations for the kingdom or God, or is it simply another way to use our children to market our churches to the community?

When we are able to practice the discipline of simplicity in our lives, we find that it brings us freedom. It brings us freedom from debt. It brings us freedom from working the long hours that separate us from our family and friends and

God. It brings us the freedom of not needing to keep up with anyone else, because we truly understand our status as the adopted sons and daughters of God, which is more than enough for a full life. We are free to be generous with what we have—money, time, and talent. Helping our kids experience this freedom is a great gift to give them. But most importantly of all, the adults in their lives must model the discipline of simplicity for them.

Simple Solitude

Solitude is another spiritual discipline that is important to develop in our children. Love for solitude can be taught to even very young children. We can help them cultivate the ability to be alone in silence in order to hear God. It's difficult to meditate or pray and to hear God if one is constantly around other people. I don't think kids these days are taught that solitude is a good thing, and they are consistently surrounded by noise—some is their own doing, and some is part of their environment. But some kids are naturals at solitude (and then I think their parents worry they are not social enough), while others are pushed into so many activities that they are hardly ever alone, except perhaps when they are asleep. And many people have difficulty being alone as they grow into adulthood. They are not good company for themselves, and they've never learned to see God as a companion.

In your children's ministry classrooms, create a solitude corner. We all know kids who aren't always ready or excited to participate immediately in large group activities. This corner should be a place where a child can go to be quiet or to separate himself from the group until he is ready to join in. Supply the solitude corner with Bible story books, simple prayer books, a finger labyrinth, or other meditation helps. Teach the children in the class that when a child is in the solitude corner, she is not to be bothered. Suggest to parents that they create a space like this at home for their family. Show them how to create a quiet space where anyone in the family can go when he or she wants to be alone or spend some time quietly with God. Parents need to teach the rest of the family to respect the silence and solitude of the person in the quiet space. Moms home during the day with young children can work to create a quiet time when no errands are run, no friends are over, and no DVDs are watched. It could be a time for the young child to quietly look at Bible story picture books, or play with puzzles or toys that recreate a Bible story.

Large group activities for children at church can incorporate silence and solitude, teaching children to enjoy the silence and aloneness as they listen for God's voice. This is also a great way to incorporate reflection into these activities and into their lives. For example, after kids have completed a Bible learning activity, allow them to find places in your children's ministry space to be alone to think about what they learned. Offer them reflective questions to get them started on this exercise, and emphasize that this is an activity they must do by themselves. Then bring them back together and allow them to talk about what they learned during these quiet reflections.

We live in such a noisy, crowded, and extroverted world that if a love and desire for solitude is not cultivated early in our children, they may never find it within themselves to make it a part of their lives.

Stepping into Service

While many of us who work with children in churches see inculcating in our children a habit of service to others and the world as important, we don't often think of it as a spiritual discipline. But there is no question that spiritual growth does result through service to others. Jesus's sacrifice on the cross for us was the most powerful illustration of that idea we could ever ask for. So how do we teach children the ethic and the discipline of self-sacrifice?

As in the other spiritual disciplines we've discussed, the values of the child's family have great influence on instilling this foundational value in the young child. If the family holds this ethic and practices it together in their lifestyle and their use of their resources, the child will know no other way of life. Other values might capture the child as he grows older and begins to establish his own identity, but I do believe that those foundational values lived with truth in the child's family stand the child in good stead for returning to those values, no matter what experimentation takes place in the teen and young adult years.

However, an ethic of service is something the church can teach children even if the family does not necessarily always teach the idea of self-sacrifice. Over the years of personally participating in youth mission trips and church-sponsored service and mission activities, I have seen sparks of understanding ignited in the children and youth who participated in these projects. I've seen kids whose parents have fast-tracked them in hopes of the good college and Harvard MBA grow up to teach school in the inner city or serve God's kingdom in an impoverished country. I think that when we teach kids how to give of themselves from an early age, how to live that ethic of self-sacrifice, we are able to spark something in them that can last a lifetime. For example, at Jacob's Well the kids throw an annual volunteer appreciation luncheon for all the adult volunteers in the church. They act as hosts and hostesses, servers, entertainers, and the setup and cleanup crew for the event. This is a great example of kids serving the church instead of being served by the church. Since the kids are the usual recipients of volunteer time and energy, providing their volunteers with a lovely evening out is a wonderful way to teach children about the importance of saying thank you and serving others.

A core value for Trinity Church in Greenwich, Connecticut, is social justice. They have been intentional about incorporating this into their children and family ministries. The church has been involved with ministries in Rwanda since the late 1990s. Each year they do a "Rwanda Project" that families participate in together. For those projects kids and families have decorated pencil boxes and schoolbags and filled them with school supplies to send to the Rwandan children. They've raised money for the purchase of goats, cows, and the building of a house. My church does similar projects for a Masai village in Kenya. The children have raised money for drought resistant goats, water tanks, and solar panels. An elder from their village visits us twice a year so the kids have the opportunity to get to know him and some details about life in his village.

Trinity Kids did another service project this year that involved parents and children together. They worked at a local community center. They helped with landscaping and planting flowers while working side by side with the families who used the services of the center. They even involved the toddlers, who potted flowers to be given to the adults in the center's senior adults programs. At my church, kids and parents have two opportunities each year to serve together. Each October they are invited to host a Halloween party for a family center in a neighboring town, and each February we host a Valentine's party for the kids at a local shelter for those fleeing domestic violence.

Practicing Faith

Upper Room Ministries has recently released a program centering around spiritual disciplines for children. It's called The Way of the Child and weaves into its curriculum many of the spiritual disciplines we've talked about in this chapter. The program is designed to accommodate a small group of children in each session. The goal is not to enroll as many children as possible.

As the children enter the room, they are greeted, are asked to remove their shoes, and sit in a circle. They are taught to follow certain rules about silence and physical movement during each session. In the opening circle, they are introduced to the day's topic or Bible story. Then they are invited to participate in a variety of learning centers set up around the room. These centers include, but are not limited to, the topics and activities of journaling, meditation, art, sewing, and our relationship to the world. Some of the centers limit the number of children who may pariticpate in them at one time, and others can accommodate an unlimited number of participants. The children spend about thirty-five minutes in the various centers and then come back together in the circle, where they are led in a meditation around the day's topic or the Bible story. Each session moves very slowly and very quietly—quite a change from most children's ministry programs.

I had the opportunity to be with a group of children's ministry directors who had been part of the group that piloted the program for the publishers. They couldn't have been more positive about the kids' response to the sessions. Some said they had to open up more sessions because they had so many kids who wanted to participate, and others said that kids were adamant about never missing a session. Other things were put on hold so kids could make it to all the sessions. This tells us that today's children are craving opportunities to slow down and be quiet.

We spend a lot of time in our culture ensuring the physical fitness of our children. From gym classes to school sports to weekday soccer and hockey leagues, we're trying to raise a generation of children that value physical activity and keeping one's body in shape. Our hope is that these disciplines, started early, will continue into adulthood. Growth through spiritual disciplines works the same way. If we involve our children in spiritual practices early, they are more likely to incorporate God's values and God's way of life into their lives as they move into adulthood.

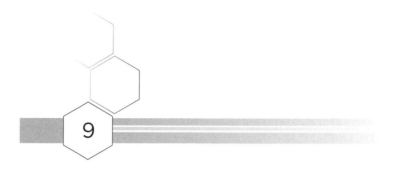

soul care through family relationships

Throughout the preceding chapters I've alluded to the family as a primary place for the spiritual nurture of the child. We've talked about the importance of family rituals and family values in the spiritual development of children. But the effectiveness of these activities and attitudes in the positive spiritual formation of the child is dependent on the quality of relationships the child experiences in the family. Christianity is a communal faith. Growth and understanding happen as we rub up against other people of faith in our communities. So if the family is the child's first community of faith, then it only stands to reason that the relationships the child experiences there are an important factor in the child growing to love God and live in the way of Jesus.

While many faithful families desire to nurture the faith of their children in real and long-lasting ways, both the form and function of today's family life and misunderstandings of what it means to pass faith on to one's children can work against positive and spiritually formative relationships in the family. Even those families who make the values of Jesus a priority for their family life can be stymied by the culture in which they are raising their children. Sometimes their best efforts at leading their children to a life of loving God and following Jesus are scattered and distracted because of everything it can take to keep life going in this culture, not to mention worries about what is really best for their children.

For example, last weekend I was speaking to a church group about today's children and how they are so connected to technology. After my talk, a dad came up to me and asked if he would be hurting the future of his children if his family didn't buy into owning all the latest technology or giving his kids the ability to text and use Twitter at an early age. Faithful families struggle with these questions, and those of us who work with families in the church need to be ready to help them find the answers that are right for their families.

From Solitary to Solid

Today's families struggle with the irregular and erratic schedules of various family members. Dad and/or Mom may be gone a significant part of the day, working to keep food on the table. The evening meal is fast food in the car as families run to a variety of afternoon and early evening commitments. These activities, which are probably good in themselves, can pull families apart rather than fuel closer relationships. Because of this increased busyness on the part of all members of the family, children can lose out on face-to-face parental relationships. As a result of this, the home is in danger of no longer being a haven of protection or a place of nurture. Instead, it has become more like an airport where children and parents pass each other on the way to their own individual activities (especially when the children are old enough to drive).

The hectic lives so many families live result in the loss of family time together, which is often replaced by individual pursuits. Children can begin to feel lonely within their own families—just the opposite of what family relationships were intended to be.[1] In fact, there have been recent news reports about the number of new homes being built with more than one play area for the children so they never have to play together or share toys with each other.

One of my guilty television pleasures is the HGTV show *House Hunters.* This reality series follows house-hunting families through a series of homes as they decide which one they would like to buy. As the families list their priorities for their new home, an individual bedroom for each child is seen as a necessity. When I was growing up, few children had their own bedrooms and television shows didn't promote it. Wally and the Beaver shared a room even though their family seemed to be well off, and the Bradys had three kids in a room. While I'm sure my fellow baby boomers would have enjoyed their own bedrooms growing up, I suspect we learned valuable lessons about living together with others because we had to share more of our lives with other family members. If families are the first places we learn how to share with others and live in right and reconciled relationships with each other, how will that ever happen if we never have to brush up against each other—even in our families?

Those of us who work with families in churches need to help families understand what it means—and the time it takes—to nurture good relationships in the family. Even the most faithful families can need coaching on what it means to develop relationships with their children that will help them form God-honoring relationships as they grow older and leave the family nest. Even the most faithful families have times when they can get caught up in life's busyness and distractions. Churches need to provide a barometer for these families to check how they are doing at building and sustaining formative relationships together. Some churches ask families to take one night a week as a family night. They often provide resources for activities the family can do together that night, such as Christian DVDs, storybooks, discussion questions, or games.

Churches need to be careful that their activities are not contributing to pulling the family apart. One family in my church scheduled their family nights for Sunday nights. Every Sunday evening the family is together and either eat a special meal together at home or go out to eat at a favorite restaurant. This year their oldest child entered high school, and our church's high school youth group meets on Sunday nights. This created a conflict for the family. They decided to change their family nights around because youth group was also a priority for the family. Even though they were able to find a way to live out both values, this family's dilemma has started an ongoing discussion within our church staff about being careful that our own programming does not interfere with the creation of these formative relationships in families.

Crashing into Culture

So much of the busyness of today's families is the result of the consumerism and competitiveness of our North American culture. The participation of some children in so many activities stems from the belief that these activities will help them be successful in life as an adult. Mom and Dad can worry that their child will be left behind if they are not participating in lots of extracurricular activities. Some of the families I work with in my church decry the expectations behind all these activities, but they have nagging worries that they are hurting their children if they don't involve them in many activities. In our churches we need to help families work through these questions. We need to help them see that alternatives are available. Find families who seem to be good at balancing family life and relationships with extracurricular activities and hold them up as models for other families to follow. Think about developing a system of mentor families where families who have worked through some of these dilemmas can help younger families who are just beginning to face these questions. Help families to see that if nurturing relationships are developed early in family life they are giving their children a foundation for spiritual and emotional success that no soccer game or dance class can ever give them.

In her book *Family, the Forming Center*, Marjorie Thompson writes about how today's consumerism and our desires for wealth and status can leave us and our families spiritually impoverished.[2] The competition in our lives blocks out the value of cooperation, which is so important to the understanding of communal relationships, both in the family and in the church. When we are constantly in competition with each other in all parts of our lives (work, school, the other mothers in the neighborhood), it's difficult to switch gears when one moves into the community of faith and live in a spirit of cooperation.

This is especially difficult for children who are just beginning to learn about the cooperation necessary in the life of a community of faith. They may wonder why outside the church they are forced into competition with their friends, but magically, when they enter the doors of the church, they must now live in love and cooperation with these same children. Because they can spend more of their time in competition than in cooperation, they are more likely to hold winning over cooperation as a value. If families are intentional about teaching cooperation and the value of reconciled relationships within themselves, and intentional about explaining to kids that always winning is not a goal of someone who lives in the way of Jesus, kids will begin to understand that living in love with others and caring for others—the ethic of self-sacrifice—is the right way to live. They will not have the pressure in their lives to be perfect and will better understand the loving forgiveness of God as they make mistakes in life and in relationships.

Churches can help families do this by not emphasizing competition in their church programs. When they don't emphasize competition with the children, they need to name it so the children begin to realize that the community of faith is a place of cooperation, love, and justice. They begin to realize that life in the community of faith is different from life in the rest of the world. Churches can teach families not to allow competition in family life, not to pit one child against another, but instead to work on forming cooperative and nurturing relationships between siblings.

Another cultural trend insidiously encroaching on families and making it more difficult for family relationships to be a positive place of spiritual nurture for children is the phenomena of the blurring of the lines between children and adults. David Elkind, a professor of child development at Tufts University, has chronicled this trend over the last twenty years or so in several of his books. Children dress like adults and are pushed into adultlike activities earlier and earlier in their lives, causing us to forget sometimes that they are still children emotionally even though they look and act so much like adults. The adult view of the child has gone from seeing the child as the innocent one who needs the help of adults to seeing the child as wholly competent in his own right.

We can see the emergence of this trend chronicled in children's literature and television shows. I'm old enough to have watched *The Andy Griffith Show* when it was new, but some of you reading this probably think of it as a historic relic you can catch on TVLand. If you watch the show carefully (and I think the same goes for another show of the same era, *Leave It to Beaver*), you'll see that Opie gets himself into a fix most times not because he is a dysfunctional child, but because he is naïve and not very sophisticated. It takes the calm, competent presence and wisdom of his father to set him straight and teach him about how the world works. In today's television programs, the children are portrayed as smarter than or more sophisticated than their parents. In these televisions shows it is the children who set their buffoonish parents straight and teach them about the world.

When we view children as more mature than they are and believe they have a sophisticated understanding of the world, this causes them to grow up faster because they are asked to shoulder more and more responsibility for themselves. When parents begin to see their kids as older and more emotionally mature than they really are, the parents may sense they can pull back from parenting, leaving the children more and more on their own to make their own decisions. Children may not feel competent to make these decisions, but because the parents give them the idea they can, they may feel it is their fault if they don't feel competent to do so. Children may feel they are letting their parents down if they are not able to live up to these expectations.

Another way this phenomena has changed family life is to equalize the importance of all family members' needs and desires. Children end up sharing authority with parents about the family's priorities and values. Parental priorities are not seen as more important than the child's, which results in the notion that everyone in the family must get to do what he or she wants or needs to do. It used to be that if Dad had to work late and Mom had a meeting in the evening, the kids' activities would take a backseat to the more pressing needs of the adults. But now, because everyone's activities are of equal importance, all sorts of juggling takes place to make sure everyone gets to do what he or she wants to do. Mom is late for her meeting or leaves her meeting early in order to pick up a child from softball practice. This subtle reordering of priorities makes it more difficult for parents to enforce their values, and the values they desire for the family, on the children.

For example, the parents may desire that the family attend church together each week, but the children have friends from families who don't hold this particular value. Therefore, many weekends out of the year the children are bombarded with invitations for Saturday night sleepovers or outings on Sundays. Because the children have subtly caught the message that their activities are as important as their parents', they find it difficult to understand why their parents often say no to these invitations that interfere with church attendance. (One commentator on the irregularity of Sunday school attendance in our churches blames sleepovers rather than sports for the problem.) This can cause conflict in the family and give parents concern about what is best for their children. They may ask themselves, "Is it really okay for me to always say no to my child's requests about Saturday night and Sunday activities?" Even faithful families may begin to doubt the importance of these foundational values they've been trying to teach their children. Persistent children can wear even the strongest parent down over time. Sometimes it helps families to have relationships with other families who hold the same foundational values. When children spend time with the children from these families, they know their values will be reinforced and not violated. And these relationships with other families can help the parents feel supported as they try to hold to their values with their children.

This equalizing of priorities and values in the family also teaches children that individual needs and desires are more important than social, public, or faith community commitments. Children begin to live into the pragmatism of doing things because of "what I can get out of it" or because of "how it makes me feel." They learn through these kinds of family relationships the opposite of the gospel ethos of Jesus. Families cannot spiritually nurture their children when they don't model characteristics of people who follow Jesus.

Growing up in a family shapes us in many ways as we watch our parents and learn from them, and as we brush up against siblings and extended family. That shaping can be both positive and negative, and most of us grow up with a mixture of both. Much of that shaping through familial relationships is about teaching children how to live, survive, and thrive in the outside world. The question for families, particularly for faithful families, is, "Which world are we preparing our children for?" Are we preparing our children for a cutthroat world where only the fittest and most aggressive survive by any means possible? Or are we preparing our children for a world where, whatever their career or professional choice, they are living by the ethic proposed by Jesus of loving one another as ourselves?

Nurturing Vital Families

All parents want their children to leave the nest and thrive. Most parents would say they would like their children to leave the world a better place. However, our actions and relationships in parenting don't always point kids toward that end. The early foundations parents lay, and the style in which they parent, in building formative relationships with their children will go a long way toward forming kids in the image of Jesus.

In their classic book *On Being Family*, Ray Anderson and Dennis Guernsey write about the role of parental relationships in the spiritual formation of the child. They posit that positive spiritual formation happens in families where love is an experienced reality. These are families where children learn to love God and others. They say, "The relationships that place demands upon our own life through daily and domestic proximity determine to a large extent our spiritual formation, either negatively or positively."[3] And there are no relationships, especially for children, that place more demand on our daily life than those in the family. If family relationships are guided by the values of love, justice, forgiveness, and reconciliation—these are the values of Jesus and the people who follow him—then those children will grow to be people who love God and love others more than themselves.

Anderson and Guernsey also say that children are spiritually formed in families where hope is modeled for them in their relationships. Children who observe lives lived for some sort of greater purpose learn that life is not dependent on personal successes and failures. When our lives are not all about us but are instead about something greater—say, working with God to bring about God's kingdom of love here on earth—then setbacks and victories are not ours, but God's. They are only part of the big picture, and not the whole picture, of our personal identities. After all, didn't Jesus talk about losing our lives in order to gain them? In order to be positively spiritually formed, to live that abundant life Jesus promised, our lives need to be about God and God's kingdom, not ourselves. When we model this in our relationships with our children, and teach this credo to our children over and over again, they will see the fruition of that promise of abundant life as well.

Anderson and Guernsey write about what they call the "vital family." A vital family is one that energizes and nurtures the abilities of both children and parents. The vital family is a place where parents practice committed, covenantal love toward each other and their children. And it is a place where authentic and authoritative parenting takes place. It is a place of high support and high control where members of the family are interdependent on each other, not independent individuals pursuing their own agendas who happen to occupy the same home. Vital families nurture family relationships conducive to the spiritual formation of their members.

So how do churches help families be these vital families? In some ways this task is beyond the scope of what any church children's ministry can hope to accomplish. It's difficult to attract parents to come to "parent training," and I'm not sure any one lecture or discussion will immediately change the direction or values of any one family. We can continue to invite families to come and learn together through worship, activities, and service projects. We can think creatively about preparing the young couples in our churches for parenthood. We can continue to provide resources to help families build strong relationships with each other and that enable parents to weave God's story into the story of their family. We can help families develop those rituals written about earlier. Churches can model good communal relationships and values for the families to emulate. As we keep at these things, making the building of strong, vital families a priority for our churches, we will begin to see families develop relationships together that spiritually nurture their children. And we'll see already faithful families become stronger.

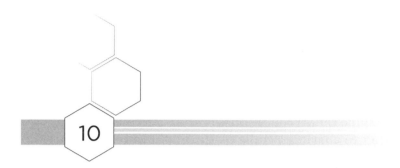

facilitating spiritual formation through community relationships

When I was a seminary student in religious education, the concept of integrating the generations within church programs was in vogue. People were talking and writing about the value of intergenerational education as if it were the "next new thing" in educational ministry. Then the whole movement fizzled out. Now in recent years this idea of bringing the generations together has reared up again, but it never seems to catch on in practical church ministry.

A few shining examples exist of some very brave churches who have bucked the trend and worked hard at bringing the generations together in their congregations, but they are few and far between. I've been successful at executing intergenerational events and some summer learning experiences that brought the generations in my church together. But for the most part, I've met roadblocks in implementing this idea of generations knowing each other, caring for each other, and learning from each other. This is a shame, I believe, because a faith community that facilitates the positive spiritual formation of its members is one where the generations know and respect each other—not one where the generations are separated from each other, with no significant relationships between them.

Why is this? Other trends have caught on and stayed with us in the church education world, so why has it been so difficult to convince people of the importance of mixing the generations together?

This is one way the church reflects our North American culture. We live in a very age-stratified culture. Children's schools and sports teams are graded by age. Movie and television producers create programming for specific age groups so the marketing people know to whom to sell the ad time. Watch the commercials on certain television shows, and you'll know who is expected to be watching. It is no coincidence that adult diapers are advertised during reruns of *Murder, She Wrote.* The church has just followed suit, creating segments of ministry that appeal to certain age groups as a way of attracting them into the church building. In fact, if you look at many church websites, one of the first things you'll see they proclaim about themselves is the strength of their children's and youth programs. They are proud of the way they separate the generations, and they understand it is a selling point to people who are looking for a new church. Perhaps we've come to believe that this is the way things are supposed to be. If that is so, then we are walking down the wrong path. Faith communities are meant to be places where we share life together and welcome all who come—not just those in our own age group or generation.

This cultural influence causes those in our churches not to want to be with other generations because they have been told they don't need to be. Our culture and media have created generational stereotypes we believe in because we don't personally know people from generations other than our own.

Older people don't want to be at events that include children, because they are convinced the children will only be noisy, undisciplined, and disruptive. Young people don't want to be with older adults, because they think they are stodgy and out of touch. And let's face it: everyone is afraid of teenagers.

Age stratification happens because we've turned the church into a place where we go for "what we can get out of it." Churchgoers don't want anything to happen that will disrupt or mar their experience. Parents who deal with their kids all week want them in the nursery or other church programs, because that hour at church is a chance for peace and quiet. Or empty nesters often have the attitude of "I had my turn doing the kid thing—now let someone else have a turn." Neither of these attitudes reflect an understanding of what living in God's family is all about.

Finally, *ageism* is a reason we fight against intergenerational relationships in the church. The ageism of our culture, the bias against people who are older, has insidiously wormed its way into our attitudes about those people older than us in our faith communities. Because we live in such a youth-oriented culture, we have become afraid of growing old. The fact that more and more people are doing more and more things to avoid looking older tells me our culture has sent a message that growing old or being old is a bad thing, an undesirable part of life. Therefore, even in the church younger people don't want to be with the older folks, because it forces them to look right into the face of their own mortality. It forces them to see that no matter how much they do to make themselves look younger and act younger, age eventually catches up with everyone. We are a people in great denial about growing old. But I don't think God wants it that way, and I don't think God is in favor of faith communities practicing or abetting covert ageism. Fostering intergenerational relationships in faith communities is one way to buck the culture of ageism.

The demographic makeup of some newer and emerging churches is often very young. They are made up of college students, young adults, and young married couples, with and without children. They are often missing a generation of memory. These communities need to be careful not to get so comfortable with each other that when an older person visits or joins that community they fail to practice hospitality and inclusiveness toward that person. The older person needs to be welcomed as a positive addition to the community, filling a generational hole in the community. These communities need to reflect thoughtfully on ways to involve their children with more experienced generations. Without those relationships, their children are missing an opportunity to hear stories from people who have followed Jesus for a long time.

As a minister, one of my favorite rites of the church in which to participate is the baptism of babies. I love leading the eager parents and their wide-eyed offspring through the vows and introducing these young children to their community of faith. But the part I love the most is when the community of faith vows to help the parents raise these children to be Christians. In one church I served, the community vows ended with the words "for they belong to us as well." To me both the vows the parents make and the vows the community makes are as important as marriage vows. After all, they are both said in a sacred space before God. God takes these vows seriously, and so should we. Every time a church community engages in the rite of baptism, it is a powerful reminder of the generational interrelatedness of God's family. And not to work to foster these relationships in other areas of church life is to unplug the rite of baptism from its power source. If your church practices infant dedication instead of baptism, the witnessing community still makes vows to assist the parents in helping the child to love God and follow Jesus. So despite the currents flowing against programs fostering intergenerational relationships in the church, churches interested in the positive spiritual formation of its members need to exert the effort to swim upstream and work to provide opportunities for the generations to learn and play together.

Creating Shared Experiences

Faith communities need to offer their diverse generations the opportunity for shared experiences. In my experience, there is no better way to build community among people than through shared experiences. Recently my church held a women's retreat at a convent not far from our church campus. About forty women attended. At least three generations were represented in the group. We were led through a variety of exercises dealing with meditation and contemplation. From all accounts, the day was an extraordinary experience for most everyone there. The next morning, a Sunday, one of the women who had been at the retreat came up to me and commented on how she felt that all the women who were at the retreat were connected in a very special way. That shared experience had brought us all together. But the thing about shared experiences is that a community needs to keep having them in order for the relationships to grow. The glow and connectedness from that retreat has faded over time, and that group has not had a chance to reconnect or to reflect on what happened that day. I'm not sure what the tipping point is that moves a group from just a great experience to a place where authentic relationships are fostered, but I know it takes more than one experience. Maybe the exact number depends on the group of people involved.

Shared experiences give people a common basis for conversation. One of the reasons that casual intergenerational events don't often produce the hoped for results is that people of different generations don't really know what to talk about with each other and are a bit intimidated by having a conversation with someone much younger or older. If a group made up of different generations has an experience in common, they have something to talk about together. Once the conversational ice is broken around this experience, the participants might just find out other things they can converse about with the others. Prompting the participants with reflective questions about the shared experience is a good way to get them talking with each other.

By their very nature, faith communities are covenantal. In the Hebrew Scriptures, connectedness among the generations is always understood in terms of covenant.[1]

> The sense of generational relatedness in covenant has been diminished in modern society by the stress on individualism. By contrast, in ancient Israel the notion of an "individual' (autonomous free agent) is virtually nonexistent. Identity was lodged in the nation of Israel.[2]

In Scripture, the passing on of faith was always done intergenerationally, informally and nonformally. The idea of generations isolated from each other was unheard of. Jesus's teaching expanded the idea of generational togetherness outside of those related to each other, which was then foundational to the cultural ethos of the early church. But in our North American zeal for individualism, we often lose sight of the fact that when we officially join a faith community, we commit to a covenant of relationship with each other—the whole community of faith, not just those who are like us or in the same age demographic.

Being the Body

Paul's description of the church as the body of Christ in the first letter to the Corinthians describes how the body needs every part; the foot needs the eyes and the fingers need the toes. The point of the whole passage is that everyone in the community of faith needs to work together and recognize the worth of each other, but somehow we've lost that when we think we can have a true community of faith without children being a visible and vital part of it. And without the generations rubbing up against each other and knowing each other, those covenantal and formational relationships will never happen.

Throughout the history of religious education, one can find an emphasis on relationships as a potent force in the spiritual growth of Christians.

> Whatever the origin of the emphasis, it is certain that contemporary Christian religious educationists stress relationships as the sine qua non of faith. Learning and growing in the religious life take place, they say primarily in the company of significant others in the family and the community of believers.[3]

We've lost this belief in the formational power of relationships in the contemporary church when it comes to children. With teachers who teach once or twice a month and children shunted off to specially designated building areas, or in some cases their own buildings, the chances for these intergenerational relationships to form are few and far between. This is unfortunate, because not only are our children losing out on being influenced by other members of the faith community, but the church is losing its seminal identity as a place where things can happen because of God's presence that don't happen in other places in the world. A church demonstrating generational unity and respect for both its elders and its children would be a powerful model to our culture of ageism.

The church is losing its unique calling—its ability to demonstrate unity and love within great diversity. When the church ceases to be the church in this way, it becomes nothing more than the local community center that just happens to tell people about Jesus. It becomes just another place where adults, teens, and children come to participate in their own interests and have their own worldviews confirmed. When the church settles for this, it concedes its ability to be a place of transformation and veers away from God's original plan for how the people of God are called to live together.

In his classic text *Intergenerational Religious Education*, James W. White writes about the importance that love plays in bringing the generations together and in promoting understanding between the generations.

> The implications of loving for the educational task are many. First, and foremost, loving is the style by which the best religious education, including intergenerational expression, is guided. These sundry persons in and around churches and synagogues are not just anybodies, who come together for worship, fellowship and learning. They are somebodies. Their becoming is more effectively enhanced by loving. . . . People are best motivated by relationships which honor and respect them as persons. Though we highly value the love received from same age peers, we also are moved by the kind of attention given by people younger and older. Few things are nicer than a child on one's lap or a shoulder rub by a grandma.[4]

I held a three-month-old baby on my lap this morning as a part of baptism preparation, and I can add an "Amen" to the above statement. Again, when we join a faith community, usually we covenant to live with each other in love. And love is attractive and contagious. After all, Jesus told his disciples that the world would know what he was all about because of the love they had for each other. Imagine a church where the generations love and take care of each other. Imagine a church where the generations have authentic relationships with each other. This would indeed be a church that showed people what it means to live in the way of Jesus. And this would indeed be a place of personal and communal transformation.

Bridging the Generations

You may be nodding your head in agreement. "I get what you are saying. But tell me what to do about it. My church just spent a million dollars creating a new children's ministry wing. I can't go to my senior pastor and tell him that I'm changing my whole philosophy of children's ministry." Or you might be in the opposite position, working with a team of ever-changing volunteers, struggling to get resources on a nonexistent budget, working with ten children who range in age from five to twelve, and trying desperately to get a church filled with college students and young single people to participate in the spiritual formation of these kids. Changing the culture of a church to promote intergenerational relationships can be a daunting task.

I once heard a story of a small church in North Dakota. The pastor of this church became convicted that the church needed to be a real community of faith that brought the generations together in learning, worship, and fellowship. He decided to make this happen. The church decided to use a curriculum that guided them through both education and worship along similar themes in contexts that kept the generations together.

When some people complained to him about this new direction, he told them that this church was going to be one where all the generations would know each other, love each other, and learn from each other. And he gently told them that if that was a problem for them, they should perhaps look for another church. Some of them did. After the struggle of implementing his plan, this pastor felt he needed to leave the church. But an interesting thing happened. After he left, that congregation didn't revert back to what they'd done before. They continued down this road of intergenerational learning and worship, despite the struggle, having seen the value in forming this type of faith community. I tell this story to show that this change can be made, but it may be difficult and costly, and different church cultures will need to process the change in different ways.

The way to begin bringing the generations together in any church is to start small and think very intentionally about it. Intergenerational ministry is far easier to implement in a small- to middle-sized church than a megachurch. Thinking intentionally about transgenerational ministry means always thinking about everything one does in children's ministry and other areas of church ministry through the grid of the generations reflected in your church. For example, at my church some of the older women had started making baby quilts to give to some local charities. For some reason, they were never finished. Someone got the idea that they should be finished, and she then invited teenage girls from our youth group to work with the older women in finishing them. So one afternoon they met in a room in our church building and finished the quilts together. The woman who pulled this group together was thinking outside of the generational box. Unfortunately, she didn't take the idea far enough, because even though the teens and older women were in the same room together, they had very little interaction with each other. We needed some way to get them talking. It's a work in progress, but the seeds of an intergenerational encounter had been sown.

Our Minister of Pastoral Care has started an annual event called the Women of Wisdom dinner. Any woman eighty or older is designated a woman of wisdom and invited to this dinner. Younger women of the faith community attend this dinner as a way of honoring the wisdom of these older women. The generations mix at the dinner tables and get to know each other during the meal. I would love to see more women bring their young daughters to this dinner to meet these women of wisdom.

I was so pleased this year when one of our older women (one of the women of wisdom) volunteered to be a small group leader at our vacation Bible camp. She worked with the fourth and fifth graders. She had a marvelous time, and these kids had the opportunity to know her in a new and special way. Don't be afraid to invite older people to be a part of the children's ministry. When I was speaking at the Willow Creek Children's Ministry Conference this spring, I met an older man who had spent several years being a greeter in Willow Creek's children's ministry. He told me with delight about the children he greeted each week. He told me about knowing their names and how they were so excited to see him each week as they made their way to Promiseland. These older people may be reluctant to join you at first, but once they try it and get into it, most will really enjoy being with and meeting the children.

Look for ways you can provide places where the generations can learn together. The first church I served as a director of Christian Education was a small church in Chicago. Because I was in charge of both the children's and adult education programs during the summer, I had the authority to cancel the age-graded Sunday school and create an intergenerational Sunday school program. Initially I thought only parents and their kids would attend, but to my surprise several older adults with no relationship to any children in the church came. I was thrilled, and we had a wonderful time together for the several summers we did this program as we explored Bible stories, acted out skits, and created craft projects together.

Churches without a lot of generational diversity need to be intentional about taking advantage of the generational diversity they do have. The formational relationships don't always need to be between a child or teen and a senior citizen. Relationships between children and younger adults are intergenerational too. These relationships can be just as spiritually forming as those with older people. Children need to be in relationship with adults of all ages in the church. They need to be able to watch closely how these people try to follow Jesus every day. They need to know that these people love them and are pleased that these children are part of their faith community. We need to rethink the ways we separate all the generations in the church and find ways to bring them together in loving relationships.

It is shameful that the generations are so separated in our churches. And it is even more of a shame that most churchgoers in this country seem to prefer it this way. Those of us interested in facilitating the spiritual nurture of children need to think seriously and intentionally about how we can bring our churches more in line with God's ideal of a covenantal community of faith. Whether it be through including children in corporate worship, building strong relationships between children and children's ministry volunteers, planning intentional intergenerational events, or creating mission experiences that involve people in different stages of life, today's churches need to act on helping their members—young, old, and in-between—find meaningful relationships with each other for the purposes of modeling the life of faith and developing a sense of belonging for all members of the faith community. Spiritual formation happens in a community made up of different kinds of people, not in an age-stratified vacuum.

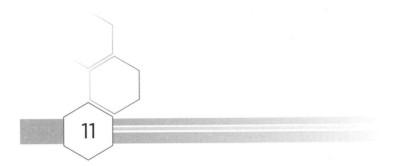

facilitating spiritual formation through peer-to-peer relationships

I grew up in the church. During my childhood this small church met in a variety of venues: a small Catholic chapel, an elementary school, a former nightclub, the basement of the parsonage, and, finally, its own building. The constant for me through those early church attendance years was my friends. My family lived about a half hour's drive from our church, so I didn't see my church friends except on Sundays and Saturday mornings for junior choir practice. Those days were the highlights of my week.

Despite spending less time with them, I recall my church friends better than the friends from my elementary school classes. I especially looked forward to the Sundays when one of them might be allowed to come home with me for the afternoon or I might be allowed to spend the afternoon at one of their houses. (In those days we went to church on

Sunday evenings too, so we could be returned to our parents without an extra trip.) Church attendance became a habitual part of my life.

As my friends and I were on the cusp of adolescence, always a turning point for childhood relationships, a new family started attending our church. They were wealthier than our families and seemed so much more sophisticated than any of us. This family had a daughter who was my age, and she lived closer to my friends than I did. She captivated them. Soon I felt like an outsider with these children who had been my best friends. As I look back on it now, I'm not really sure what happened. Maybe I was wrong to blame it all on the new girl—perhaps it was simply what would have happened to our friendships as we headed into the turbulent teen years. But no matter what, the bottom line was that I was very hurt and felt ostracized by these girls with whom I had spent most of my childhood. A casualty of this rift was that I no longer felt the same affection for church attendance that I once did. Part of this might also have been due to the onset of puberty, but I know that the seeming loss of these friendships had something to do with the jettisoning of my faith during my teenage years.

The church I currently serve in has a very large youth group. Many of the kids are not from families who attend our church. The reason they attend is because our youth group has a reputation for helping these kids develop caring and loving relationships with each other, devoid of the competition and cliques that populate our local high school. These kids feel they can come to youth group and not have to put on the masks and affectations they feel the need to put on in school. They feel they can come and be part of this group, be themselves, and be friends with kids their groups at school would not allow them to be friends with. This acceptance, these friendships, are the main reason these kids are a part of our church.

Helping kids to build friendships with other kids in your faith community is an important piece of their spiritual formation. Both church educators and parents have a role to play in helping this happen. But I see a number of obstacles that stand in the way of our kids building solid peer relationships in the faith community.

The Challenges

The first obstacle is the irregular attendance of many of our kids. Whether we blame it on less committed families, sports, single-parent and blended families, or Saturday night slee-povers, the fact is that most of our children are not in our church programs each and every week. One of the things that built my childhood friendships was that, unless I was sick, I was at church every single Sunday, as were my friends. I know times have changed since then, but the fact that friendships are built through physical proximity has not. So if a child is always with different children whenever he attends church programs, he will never develop peer friendships in the community of faith.

Second, the larger our children's programs become, the more difficult it is for children to have the opportunity to build friendships with other kids. I've often thought about writing an article about why big churches are bad for the spiritual nurture of children. The larger the group of children, the easier it is for a child, particularly the shy or quiet or less-charismatic child, to get lost in the crowd. Creating small groups out of the large group helps to mitigate this somewhat. But as large churches struggle to recruit enough volunteers, often these small groups are not all that small. For some children, simply walking into a room filled with fifty to one hundred other children can be an intimidating experience. Large churches need to put lots of intentionality around helping kids build relationships with each other. Many large churches work hard at helping the adults build relationships. The same intensity needs to be given to children's relationships as well.

The third obstacle is that many parents don't pay a lot of attention to what is happening in the children's education program. The less parents know about what is happening, the less they are going to know the families and kids in their child's age group at church. Large churches may have many different schools and school systems represented in each class, which means that the only time these kids see each other is on Sundays or at other church activities. At my church, most of the kids live in the same town and attend the public schools, but with three elementary schools in town and some kids in private school, the kids still don't always see each other outside of church activities. Churches facing the problem of kids from many school systems could let parents know what other kids attend from their neighborhood or town, or they could think about building their small groups around certain geographic areas or school systems.

A fourth obstacle for many emerging churches is the lack of children, and therefore children's ministries. While many emerging churches are doing interesting things, there can still be a lack of peer-to-peer relationships simply because there are very few "peers" for many of the elementary and middle school children. I know emerging churches where there are thirty or more children under the age of five, but fewer than ten children in the elementary and middle school stage. This can lead to a sense of loneliness and isolation for those children who have no peers to connect with. And that can lead those children to find church boring and irrelevant. The challenge for such churches is keeping these children involved and engaged in the life of the community.

These obstacles—and you might have others at play in your community—work against our efforts to help children build meaningful peer-to-peer relationships in the context of the community of faith. Yet this concept is important enough to their spiritual formation that we can't just throw our hands in the air and say it just can't happen. We need to figure out ways to help this process along despite the obstacles.

The Benefits

These peer-to-peer relationships in the faith community are important for several reasons. The knowledge that their friends will be present will help kids enjoy coming to church and help them build the habit of being part of a community of faith. If you've ever moved to a new community and taken on the task of trying to find a new church to attend, you'll understand how difficult it is to motivate yourself to go to a gathering where you don't know anyone. I have had this experience, and it was not a process I enjoyed. I hated walking into a place where I didn't know a soul and everyone else seemed to know each other and what to do. I disliked it so much that it took me a long time to find a faith community. Some Sundays I didn't attend church because I loathed the whole process. If kids are faced with the prospect of being dropped off in a setting where they know no one, are unfamiliar with the routine, and no effort is made to help them make friends, they are not going to want to be there week after week. And if they aren't there, they will be missing the important communal and relational piece of their spiritual formation.

As children grow, we know that the influence of the peer group becomes more and more important in the child's life. It would be great if some of the child's peer relationships were with other kids who have been involved in the same processes of transformation and spiritual formation. As the influence of peers grows on, the child will have at least some friends who hold the same foundational values. I don't think all of the child's peer relationships should fit that category, but I hope that some of them will.

Much of a child's healthy emotional development is dependent upon being accepted by other children. All of us know the sting of hurtful things done to us by other children. To some extent this is just a part of growing up. However, the more we can do to facilitate friendships and acceptance in our church programs, the more helpful and successful we will be in facilitating healthy emotional and spiritual development in our children. If a child only knows church as a hurtful place, he will never want to be part of a faith community as he grows older. And when we help kids develop healthy relationships with each other, we are teaching them about what it means to live in community. We are teaching them about the inclusiveness and acceptance inherent in the kingdom of God, and that this is how people who follow Jesus live.

Nurturing Friendships

All of us who work with children in the church need to first make sure we are exhibiting the inclusiveness and acceptance of God's kingdom to these children. Here are some questions to ask yourself and those working with the children:

- Do we know all their names? It's difficult to introduce children to each other if we don't know who they are. I've discovered that, apart from preschoolers, keeping name tags on children for an extended period of time takes vigilance and intentionality. Still, it's worth it. Being able to call children by name helps them to feel they belong in the group and helps them to begin to know the other children.
- Are we excited about seeing each and every child when they walk through the door each week? I know we all have kids in our programs whom we struggle to like and relate to. They might be difficult and uncooperative, or they might not fit in with the rest of the class. The other children may not like them either. We need to exhibit acceptance of these children in the same way we exhibit it to the kids we naturally like. Otherwise we won't be modeling the right attitude to the kids in our programs. When kids see us accepting these less-

than-likable children, perhaps they will become more accepting as well.

- Are we aware of the kids in our programs and classes who don't seem to know the other kids or seem to be left alone by the other kids? With these kids we need to be proactive, introducing them to other kids (maybe those who go to the same school, live in the same neighborhood, or have the same interests) and helping the whole class include them in their activities and conversations. Modeling inclusion and acceptance is in some ways more important than making sure every jot and tittle of the lesson is covered.

There are other things we can do as the adults in a child's life—whether parents or teachers or extended family—to help kids develop friendships and learn how to be good friends with others. Helping children to develop empathy, the feelings and points of view of others, will go a long way toward helping them develop into caring friends and people who live in the way of Jesus. Give children the opportunity to develop the skills of cooperation and problem solving. Whenever we play a game in the classroom or ask them to work together in a group on a project, we are helping them develop these skills, especially when we step into situations where these skills are not being demonstrated and guide them in the proper direction. Encourage children to show support and appreciation for others. Teach kids to say "please" and "thank you" to other kids, and to ask how people are while really caring about the answer.

Talking with children about how they treat their friends provides a great opportunity for talking about the way Jesus said we should treat other people. It's a serious opportunity to teach them about making the choice to treat others in the same way they would like to be treated. If there is a child in the class or the neighborhood everyone makes fun of and is never included in games and activities, this is an even better time for a lesson about what it means to be a person who follows Jesus in terms of how we treat this person.

Children can learn from each other what it means to be a lover of God and a follower of Jesus. Children teach each other things all the time. They teach each other how to play video games, how to work with computer programs, how to execute a soccer kick—yet we hardly ever think about what they can teach each other about faith. As we encourage kids to talk about their experiences with God, their friends and the other children will listen to them and learn about ways to experience God too. When other kids demonstrate and model a desire to live in the way of Jesus in front of their friends, their friends may be interested in doing the same thing.

Parents can be intentional about helping their children form peer-to-peer friendships in the community of faith. They can get to know other families in the community who have children the same age as their own, perhaps spending time with them outside of church programs and events. They can invite church friends as well as school friends to birthday parties. Of course, this means that parents need to know who the other children are in their child's age group at the church programs.

Young children don't really understand the concept of friendship until around first or second grade. But when they reach fifth grade, the group or clique becomes all important. Parents and other adults lose influence as the peer group expands in importance. This underscores the importance of helping our kids form friendships at an early age with kids who share their values and who are good influences, and of providing environments where those relationships can develop. And because we want our kids to also have friends who don't necessarily share their values—this is part of what it looks like to be a Jesus follower—we also need to help them learn how to stand up for their own values, teach them that they are lovable and competent, and teach them how to value the views of others while still living by the values of Jesus. We must teach them how to love their neighbors.

And we need to help them understand the biblical concept of community. While they may not have an affinity for friendship with every person they meet in their faith community, they are still bound to love them, care for them, and work in cooperation with them. Stressing the living of just and right relationships with children from an early age will help them do this.

For all the social challenges children in smaller churches face, there are some ways we can capitalize on the intimacy of these communities. Children in smaller churches may be able to develop relationships with children who are slightly older or younger than they are. This gives the older children the opportunity to be a model of what it means to be a friend for the younger kids, and gives the younger children the opportunity to learn from older kids about good relationships. If they are involved in multiage classes, they have the opportunity to serve the younger kids by helping them with the projects or the games. And they have the opportunity to experience service as they are served in the same way by the older kids. This kind of setting can also teach them about how to build relationships with those who are not exactly like them.

Smaller churches might think about how to use the few children they have in the full life of the church. These churches can think creatively about ways to use them in the worship service and ways to use them in other ministries of the church, such as hospitality and missional service. This will provide natural opportunities for these children to build nurturing relationships across generational lines. Churches lacking large numbers of children need to put more emphasis on helping the children they do have develop cross-generational relationships.

Another benefit to a small number of children is that those who work with these kids have the chance to build real connections with them. While these aren't the same as peer-to-peer relationships, they can be a tremendous blessing to children who are often overlooked in larger communities. As you get to know the children in your community, you can begin to plan activities that draw on what you know about them and their strengths, interests, and challenges.

These churches also might find that they need to be more open to visiting children so that elementary and middle schoolers feel welcomed in bringing their friends with them to church activities. We need to be as engaged with these visitors as we would be with the children we see every week, learning their names, showing enthusiasm at their presence, taking the time to catch up when we haven't seen them for a while. And we need to recognize that these children are never to be seen as a means by which we can get their parents to become part of our churches. Children are not tools for church growth. By planning activities that can be done by a small class or a large group, by making room for guests and building deeper relationships with these children, leaders can help even the lone ten-year-old feel valued and connected in his faith community.

Positive friendships help kids learn about living with others well, and help them live well in the world. These skills transfer easily to living in community with others and becoming a person who loves God and follows Jesus.

afterword

During the writing of this book my appendix ruptured and I rushed myself to the hospital, where I had emergency surgery. I spent a week in the hospital on an IV antibiotic drip to combat the infection in my body. Gradually, the realization that this episode could have resulted in my death has come over me. I had no excruciating pain. I thought I'd eaten some bad sushi or had an odd case of the stomach flu. I could have ignored this, because I have a high tolerance threshold for illness. Had I ignored it, I would have died. This realization has not been what I'd call a life-changing epiphany, but I sense there is a difference in the way I understand the way my life works. I know I need to stop putting things off that I think are important or would like to do. And I know that I need to continue to practice the ideas talked about in this book because the stakes are too high not to. And I know that to choose to ignore the problem in the way we do children's ministry in our churches is to ensure its death.

When we talk about facilitating the spiritual formation of our children, we desperately need to think outside the box. We need to redefine and rework all that we do in churches with our children and families. I don't have all the answers, but I hope the preceding pages have continued the discussion begun in *Postmodern Children's Ministry*. I hope the ideas have sparked and captured your imagination. I hope they have wormed their way into your heart and soul as you think about caring for the children in your faith communities. I hope you, too, see the urgency in remaking our understanding of children in the church in this country.

I pray that God speaks to some of you through this book, some of you far more creative than I, who will have the courage to stand up and say, "Everything must change." If we are really serious about capturing the imaginations of our children for the kingdom of God, we do have to change the way we do our business. And we have to speak to faithful families about the way they do theirs.

Godspeed in your dedication to the children in your faith communities and your families. May God bless your efforts and bring forth the fruit of God's kingdom.

notes

Introduction

1. Brian J. Walsh and Sylvia C. Keesmaat, *Colossians Remixed: Subverting the Empire* (Downers Grove, IL: InterVarsity, 2004).

Chapter 2 The Child and God's Story

1. Mark Yaconelli, *Contemplative Youth Ministry* (Grand Rapids: Zondervan, 2006), 207.

2. Hans W. Frei, *The Eclipse of Biblical Narrative* (New Haven, CT: Yale University Press, 1980), 130, as quoted in John W. Wright, *Telling God's Story* (Downers Grove, IL: InterVarsity, 2007), 50.

3. Wright, *Telling God's Story*, 51.

4. Ibid.

5. "Millennials," or "Generation Y," are the generation born between 1982 and 2003. They are all in elementary school and older. "Futuristic adaptives," or "Generation Z," are the generation born from 2003 forward.

6. Catherine M. Wallace, "Storytelling, Doctrine and Spiritual Formation," *Anglican Theological Review* 81 (1999): 39–59 (also available at www.catherinem wallace.com).

7. Charles Foster, *Educating Congregations: The Future of Christian Education* (Nashville: Abingdon, 1994).

Chapter 3 The Child and the Story of God's Church

1. Chris Armstrong, "The Future Lies in the Past," *Christianity Today*, February 2008, 22–29.

2. Ibid.

3. Thomas Cahill, *How the Irish Saved Civilization* (New York: Anchor, 1996).

4. Harold Myra, *Santa, Are You for Real?* (Nashville: Thomas Nelson, 1997).

Chapter 5 The Child and the Story of Faith

1. Karen-Marie Yust, *Real Kids, Real Faith: Practices for Nurturing Children's Spiritual Lives* (San Francisco: Jossey-Bass, 2004), 65.

Chapter 6 The Transformative Power of Ritual

1. Randall Collins, *Interaction Ritual Chains* (Princeton, NJ: Princeton University Press, 2005), 8.

2. Robert Bococh, *Ritual in Industrial Society: A Sociological Analysis of Rituals in Modern England* (London: Allen and Unwin, 1979), 37.

3. Collins, *Interaction Ritual Chains*, 36.

4. Ibid., 37.

5. Ibid.

6. Ibid., 39.

7. Ibid.

8. Ibid., 39–40.

9. Brett P. Webb-Mitchell, *Christly Gestures* (Grand Rapids: Eerdmans, 2003), 214.

10. Gertrude Mueller Nelson, *To Dance with God: Family Ritual and Community Celebration* (New York: Paulist, 1986), 400.

11. Friesen, "Rituals and Family Strength," *Direction Journal* 19 (Spring 1990): 39–48.

12. Ibid.

13. Ibid., 11.

14. Nelson, *To Dance with God*, 25.

15. Marjorie Thompson, *Family, the Forming Center*, rev. and exp. ed. (Nashville: Upper Room, 1997), 89.

Chapter 7 Children in the Worshiping Community

1. As I first began exploring the spiritual formation of children in the postmodern context of the twenty-first century, I wrote and talked about the importance of involving children in the communal, corporate worship of the church because worship was, in itself, an act of spiritual formation. Several years ago I was at an Emergent convention in San Diego, and my friend Brian McLaren taught a workshop on the subject. I'm indebted to Brian for what follows and for expanding my understanding of this important topic.

Chapter 8 Facilitating Spiritual Formation through Spiritual Disciplines

1. Richard Foster, *Celebration of Discipline* (San Francisco: HarperSanFrancisco, 1988), 29.

2. Ibid., 30.

Chapter 9 Soul Care through Family Relationships

1. I am indebted to David Elkind's book *Ties That Stress: The New Family Imbalance* (Cambridge, MA: Harvard University Press, 1998) for this discussion.

2. Thompson, *Family, the Forming Center*, 48.

3. Ray Anderson and Dennis Guernsey, *On Being Family* (Grand Rapids: Eerdmans, 1985), 123–24.

Chapter 10 Facilitating Spiritual Formation through Community Relationships

1. James W. White, *Intergenerational Religious Education* (Birmingham, AL: Religious Education, 1988), 70.

2. Ibid., 70.

3. Ibid., 132.

4. Ibid., 85.

Ivy Beckwith holds a religious education degree from Gordon-Conwell Theological Seminary and a PhD from Trinity Evangelical Divinity School. She is an ordained minister who has served numerous congregations in the Midwest and on the East Coast. She has also worked as an editor and education consultant for Group Publishing and Gospel Light Publications. She currently serves the Congregational Church of New Canaan, Connecticut, as the Minister for Children and Families. She also works with churches as a consultant and speaker in the areas of staff hiring, staff development, and children's ministry evaluation. She is the author of *Quick Relief for Children's Ministry Leaders*, *Postmodern Children's Ministry*, and *The Ultimate Survival Guide for Children's Ministry Workers*.